THE COMPLETE GUIDE TO

PERFORMANCE STANDARDS FOR LIBRARY PERSONNEL

CAROL F. GOODSON

Neal-Schuman Publishers, Inc.

New York   London

Published by Neal-Schuman Publishers, Inc.
100 Varick Street
New York, NY 10013

With the assistance of the State University of West Georgia
Library Performance Appraisal and Revision Committee

Printed and bound in the United States of America

Library of Congress Cataloging-in-Publication Data

Goodson, Carol F.
  The complete guide to performance standards for library per-
sonnel / by Carol F. Goodson.
        p.   cm.
  Includes bibliographical references and index.
  ISBN 1–55570–262–7
  1. Library employees—Rating of—United States. 2. Librarians—
Rating of—United States. I. Title. II. Title: Performance standards
for library personnel.
  Z682.28.G66   1997
  023'.9—dc21   97–10820

This book is dedicated to Mark McManus, Interim Director, and to my fellow members of the Performance Appraisal Review and Revision Committee at the State University of West Georgia Library. Mark gave us the charge and told us to run with it, and so we have. The P.A.R.R. Committee has been a close-knit team from the very beginning, and many of the standards included in this book are the outcome of prolonged discussion within the group. Above all, Mark's willingness to entrust us with this major responsibility has allowed all of us to grow professionally and personally in ways we never imagined.

Contents

Figures

Preface

Probably no other area of administration causes more anxiety—for both supervisor and supervisee—than performance appraisal. Indeed a recent article in *Personnel Journal*[1] reported on a survey of 218 corporations that revealed widespread discontent with the employee evaluation process. A whopping 73 percent of survey respondents had either completely revamped their employee evaluation process within the past two years or planned to do so very soon. Apparently the strongest force driving this trend is the fact that more and more often salary increases depend on performance. Because of this trend, employees now, more than ever, must be assured that the appraisal process is objective, fair, and accurate.

Although it usually takes awhile for corporate stresses to find their way into nonprofits, it is clear that, as the public demand for accountability increases and the competition for the diminishing pool of funds available for merit increases escalates, more and more libraries are experiencing the same pressures as businesses.

The Complete Guide to Performance Standards for Library Personnel is predicated on two beliefs. First, that most people working in our libraries sincerely want to do the best job possible. Secondly, that most managers truly want to help everyone achieve the best level of library service. When supervisors and employees agree in advance on what standards describe that service, it is much easier to initiate a discussion about where improvement is needed and to point to specific examples of work that demonstrate the need for improvement. The mere fact that such standards exist can also help defuse tension and eradicate the complaints about favoritism or scapegoating that often surface when performance appraisals are given.

This *Guide* offers both an approach to staff evaluation and actual performance standards for a wide variety of library positions that can be used by any type of library. Both professional and paraprofessional positions—e.g., reference librarian, cataloger, bookkeeper, serials assistant—found in (and needed by) almost every library are included. To facilitate its use as a "Complete" guide, this book is organized as follows:

- Chapter 1 explains what performance standards are, how staff evaluation got to where it is today, legal issues which have impacted the process, and some recent management trends which have helped escalate the drive towards objective performance appraisal. Tips for staying out of trouble and saving supervisor and employee time are included.
- Chapter 2 recommends a process for introducing this kind of change in your library and discusses approaches for dealing with the nitty-gritty issues (e.g., "What is Average?") that will arise once you start using objective performance appraisal.
- Chapters 3 and 4 are the "meat" of the book—real performance standards modeled on ones that have been used successfully in libraries across the country.
- The final chapter is an extensive annotated bibliography of materials I read in preparation for writing this book. In a departure from the usual practice, I have included both good and not-so-good sources to help others avoid the time and effort of accessing materials that sound good in indexes or abstracts, but which upon reading, turn out to be not so useful.

The included performance standards are intentionally detailed, but not all standards will apply in every library, and individual libraries will want to add other standards. The intent of these model standards is to facilitate the manager's job of spelling out *precisely* what a library job entails and the tasks that need to be accomplished. Because of the complexity of most library jobs today (reference assistants deal with multiple formats and WebMaster performance appraisal is truly a virtual experience), each grouping includes a mixture of measurable standards, qualitative standards, and task descriptions. Some libraries will want to go further by replacing existing nebulous job descriptions with their newly adapted and augmented performance criteria.

A thread that runs through all of the more than 100 pages of detailed performance standards in this book is improved library service. For different positions, that improved service might be articulated in the standards as books shelved, cataloging turnaround time, or the time before claims are filed for missing government documents. Keeping service quality in mind is the key to selling performance standards to both library employees and higher administrators.

Because developing standards is hard work, I encourage you to share any standards you develop with the wider library community. Hopefully, the next generation of library managers will have an extensive body of literature to draw on.

NOTE

1. G. Flynn. "Employee Evaluations Get So-so Grades." *Personnel Journal* 74 (June 1995): 21–23.

1. Were the "Good Old Days" Really *That* Good?

In this chapter, you will read about what performance standards are and why they are needed; the history of performance evaluation, and the impact of the Civil Rights movement on the process; legal issues related to employee appraisal; and the connection between performance criteria and total quality management (TQM).

Undoubtedly it is only a fairy tale, but many of us in supervisory positions seem to share a belief that "once upon a time," in some halcyon days of the past, the American work ethic was such that objective performance standards for library workers—or indeed, any workers—were not needed. In that far-off, mythical time before we can remember, the fantasy story in the back of our minds goes something like this: In the good old days, people knew what they were supposed to do at work, and they did it; back then, they did their jobs without prodding, without pleading—and certainly without spending hours agonizing over an annual appraisal. If there was one at all, it had categories like punctuality, initiative, enthusiasm, creativity, and personal hygiene. And best of all, you—the department head, director, branch librarian, or whatever—were the boss—a respected and unquestioned authority, who never had to consult with your staff before making decisions, or justify to them why you did what you did.

We like to think that in those days, on the rare occasions when the supervisor felt it necessary to chastise a worker, the individual accepted the correction calmly and tried hard to do better. The managers of that day, we imagine, certainly never had to worry that a disciplined worker might return the next day with a gun! Or, if it became necessary to release someone from employment, because he or she "just didn't work out," you didn't stop to (1) verify that the unsatisfactory employee's personnel file contained a sufficient number of years' worth of negative documentation that would hold up in court, (2) make sure your own personal liability insurance was up to date, and then (3) wait to be contacted by the fired worker's attorneys.

No, in that idyllic era, "performance standards" as we now know them had not yet been invented. Today, however, things are decidedly different. In our litigious era, there seem to be no barriers preventing an employee from declaring him or herself a victim of an unfair supervisor, and finding every possible excuse for escaping his or her own responsibility for failing to meet the needs of a position or an institution.

To be completely candid about it, we must admit that some supervisors certainly are unfair. Performance standards can serve as the worker's only bulwark against discrimination in all its ugly forms: racial, religious, gender, sexual preference, and so on. When the employee has the means to demonstrate clearly that the established standards are being fulfilled or exceeded, then there is no just cause for censure or dismissal. Thus, the worker has a place to stand, a place that can be defended legally if necessary. It is just as likely, however, for an inadequate employee to hide successfully behind a history of favorable appraisals if the institution has not taken these seriously enough and seen to it that they are conducted fairly, accurately, and rigorously.

BUT ARE THINGS REALLY ALL THAT BAD?

I have begun with the negative reasons for performance standards, because I believe that in truth, such systems were created precisely because of the problems to which I have alluded. Experience has shown, however, that performance standards—if designed to reflect accurately the tasks associated with successful performance of a job, and if developed in full consultation with the workers involved—can have great benefits as well.

If you are the optimistic sort, you believe that people basically act in good faith, and sincerely want to improve. With objective performance standards, supervisors have a mechanism designed to help make that happen. When the supervisor and employee have agreed in advance on the standards, it is much easier to initiate a discussion about where improvement is needed and to point to specific examples. Alternatively, objective performance standards can be used to justify differing evaluations among staff members: the fact that such standards are in place can help immeasurably to defuse tension and quiet complaints of favoritism when the annual merit increases are distributed.

Furthermore, the staff member who is part of the performance standard development process can creatively shape the job, at least to some degree, in ways that will maximize his or her own contributions to the organization, by taking full advantage of personal strengths. Not only does this benefit the library, it obviously promotes the welfare of the individual by permitting him or her to be happier and more productive.

A "LITE" HISTORY OF PERFORMANCE STANDARDS

The basic concept of performance appraisal, although apparently a twentieth-century obsession, is not new. In

China, during the third century A.D., members of the Wei dynasty were evaluated by an "Imperial Rater." Even then, his subjective appraisals were held up for criticism, because, like some supervisors even in our enlightened era, he rated highest those he liked![1]

Much later, in 1780, the editors of the *Dublin Review* issued a method of gauging the effectiveness of members of the Irish legislature, and thus they are credited with the first modern rating system.[2] Only 33 years after that, in reputedly the earliest formal personnel evaluation, General Lewis Cass of the U.S. Army supplied the War Department with a report in which he described individual members of his regiment in such vivid terms as "good-natured" or "despised by all."

Americans will not be surprised to learn that, by 1842, the quasi-military, highly bureaucratic U.S. Civil Service was among the pioneers in what was then called efficiency rating, when the Congress decreed that the head of each department was thenceforth required to submit an annual employee service report. It was not long before local governments followed, then private industry (the department store, Lord & Taylor, began a program in 1913 which is thought to be the first).

The advent of personnel psychology after World War I, however, was responsible for the spreading of performance evaluation as we now know it. Systems of merit ratings were developed and were used to document employee progress and to fulfill other human resource management needs, such as determining promotions and setting raises and bonuses.

Prior to 1960, performance evaluations were almost exclusively used by management in order to establish administrative control; since then, however, they are used increasingly for planning, employee development, and improvement of the work environment, and to increase productivity. Even more recently, the advent of the Equal Employment Opportunity Commission stimulated interest in performance evaluations that could serve as both a way to protect organizations from lawsuits and to help ensure that diversity in the workforce is real and effective.[3]

Appraisals are normally conducted top down: that is, lower and mid-level managers are evaluated and they evaluate others under them, while upper level managers are often not subject to any form of appraisal. This situation is, however, certainly changing as peer evaluations and employee evaluations of supervisors become increasingly common.

The Equal Employment Opportunity Commission

The Equal Employment Opportunity Commission was created in response to more than 20 years of pressure by civil rights activists; it was preceded by FDR's Fair Employment Practices Committee (1941–1946) and several other unsuccessful legislative efforts during the Truman administration. By the time John F. Kennedy came along, the public was sufficiently sensitized to the need to take firm steps to rectify America's long-standing history of racial discrimination in employment, and so in 1961 President Kennedy established by executive order an Equal Employment Opportunity *Committee*, headed by Lyndon Johnson. Its charge was to root out every trace of discrimination in government employment and contracts.

The successes of the Civil Rights movement ensured that when legislation was once again introduced to create a government agency devoted to fair employment, it finally passed; the Equal Employment Opportunity Commission (EEOC) as we now know it was established in 1965.

The functions of the EEOC are mainly to enforce any federal legislation that prohibits employment discrimination, to oversee affirmative action plans, and to handle complaints about employment discrimination. Originally it handled only cases brought by federal workers, but the Equal Employment Opportunity Act of 1972 expanded authority into the private sector.[4]

Although the EEOC has from the beginning been a source of controversy on many fronts, including charges of mismanagement, criticism for enormous case backlogs, and charges that it pushed its authority beyond what Congress had intended, it has undoubtedly had a dramatic influence on personnel procedures in all kinds of workplaces and on every level. Although the EEOC does not regulate or mandate performance appraisals, its very existence changed the culture of employment practice by making supervisors overtly aware of the issue of discrimination; previously, employers often hired and fired at whim, without taking into account much beyond their personal preferences.

Because of the perception that the EEOC had a long arm, management actions that were formerly subject to little or no public scrutiny began to be considered potential bases of lengthy, embarrassing, and expensive lawsuits. The expectation has become that employees must be evaluated on reasonable standards of which they have been informed in advance, and the standards must be as objective as possible so that discriminatory actions can be avoided. Discipline or dismissal must be based on job performance and nothing else, and every effort must be made to give workers fair warning of problems and to provide ample opportunities to improve or receive needed training if appropriate.

A Little Litigation History

So, prior to the advent of the EEOC, employers assumed that they could pretty much hire, dismiss, or promote staff without restriction. Decisions affecting the lives and economic survival of employees could be made for good reasons, no reasons, or bad reasons—there was basically no control whatever.[5]

Since the passage of the Equal Pay Act in 1963 and various other federal laws that followed (e.g., the Civil Rights Act of 1964), however, there has been a tremendous increase in employment litigation. Because the courts almost always accept as evidence the performance appraisals of the employee-defendant—and these evaluations are frequently the only evidence by which a jury can decide the case—performance appraisal systems must be carefully designed so that they not only accurately measure employee performance, but can also withstand legal tests. Such challenges sometimes come when least expected, and can have devastating effects on an organization. Although the risk of such a court challenge within any specific institution is relatively slight, the financial and emotional consequences to the institution, even if the case is successfully defended, are enormous[6] and well worth avoiding whenever possible.

In order to contest successfully an appraisal that has resulted in an adverse personnel decision, the plaintiff must prove that a law protecting a specific group has been violated; it is not enough to show that the appraisal system is inaccurate if it has been *applied equally to all employees.* And therein lies the rub: that is, the issue of promotions—who gets them and who doesn't—is the area in which many successful legal challenges have been made. In order to distribute promotions safely, accurate and objective performance appraisals are crucial, because if confronted, the employer must be able to prove either that the person advanced had demonstrably superior qualifications, or that the one who was passed over for promotion was significantly inferior. The problem with most employee appraisal systems, however, is that either the standards used are not specific enough to distinguish fairly and accurately among employees, or that supervisors do not take enough care in doing the evaluations in the first place, so the ratings are inherently unfair simply *because* they are inaccurate.

One often-cited case is that of *Price Waterhouse v. Ann B. Hopkins*, in which Hopkins successfully sued her employer on the basis of sexual discrimination. She had been rejected for a partnership because of informal and subjective evaluations of her interpersonal skills. The Supreme Court agreed that her evaluators' low estimate of her was influenced by their stereotypical attitudes about how women should behave. Had the evaluation stressed job performance, the story might have ended quite differently.

Review of many legal challenges to job appraisal promotion outcomes suggests that the courts generally accept employers' definitions of acceptable job performance and their own internal assessments of which aspects are most relevant and should thus be tracked for promotion decisions. Nevertheless, those systems that have been based on a thorough job analysis, and are thus more objective, are less likely to be the subject of successful litigation by angry employees. Furthermore, courts appear to be inclined to accept a record of regular evaluations, even if done more frequently than required, as evidence that the employer tried to help the employee improve—by providing extra feedback on the employee's inadequate job performance.

In the case of dismissal of an unsatisfactory employee, it is very important that the organization attempting to defend its actions in court provide documentation of specific instances of inadequate or deteriorating job performance. In *Brown v. U.S. Steel Corporation*, for example, the company was able to fight off a charge of racial discrimination because it offered an adequate record of definite dates on which employees had been written up for tardiness, proving that there was no pattern of discrimination against Brown. The evaluative measure used—whether the employee arrived on time for work or not—was strictly objective and thus eminently determinable. Although most performance standards a supervisor would like to establish are rarely so simple, the goal of clear impartiality is definitely one to be sought. Whenever dismissal is challenged, the employers who win are those who have documentation, and can demonstrate that nonperformance of specific job requirements is the true reason the individual was terminated. It is impossible to stress this enough: the most powerful legal weapon an employer can give to an unsatisfactory employee is a record of good appraisals[7] provided by supervisors who were either too lazy to do them carefully, too cowardly to confront the employee with the truth, or too inept to recognize the risk in which they were placing their institution.

Experts on these issues agree that legal challenges to performance appraisal systems that are used to establish merit pay decisions are on the increase. In *Susan Faust v. Hilton Hotels*, the disgruntled Faust successfully argued that she received a lower salary than other executives who managed smaller operations and had poorer performance appraisals than she did. Although employers are not obligated to give the same merit increase to those who have the same performance rating, they must be able to explain differences by citing circumstances that justify the decision.[8]

STAYING OUT OF TROUBLE

To avoid the pitfalls described above, follow these recommendations:

- Redesign your performance standards on the firm foundation of a thorough job analysis of each position, preferably begun by asking the *employee* to write down what he or she actually does.

- Establish a formal, scheduled process that is the same or similar for all employees. Remind the staff well in advance when the deadline for evaluations is coming up, so that they have time to consider their own self-evaluations carefully. Good self-evaluations not only give the employee the opportunity for meaningful input, they also reduce the demand on managers who supervise many staff members.

- Be sure that all staff members know and understand the performance standards on which they will be evaluated; ideally, they should help write their own standards and agree to them in advance.

- Evaluate individuals on precise examples of job performance, not broad statements covering many tasks, which can easily be misunderstood, be misinterpreted, or allow employees to ignore some parts of their job they may not like.

- Express performance standards in terms of the behavior expected, not on the inner attitude that you hope will accompany the task!

- Whenever possible, get broad input into evaluations, including, for example, input from clientele served, coworkers, and counterparts in other organizations with which the employee has contact.

- Consider giving employees the option of submitting a portfolio with their self-evaluation, containing items that help document their own ratings of their performance.

- Any evaluation that is much above or below standard must be justified with documented evidence, either from the employee or the supervisor.

- Establish reasonable appeals procedures and deadlines for filing appeals for those who are not satisfied with their evaluations.

- Although supervisors doing evaluations must be instructed in how to implement the system consistently, discrepancies between departments are inevitable, so a review committee should be established to examine all the evaluations together and rectify any patterns of inequity across the whole organization.

- Conduct performance evaluations at least annually, and allow for periodic negotiation (at least every six months) between employee and supervisor. In today's work climate, job responsibilities and institutional needs can change quickly, and it is only fair that employees be evaluated for what they are really doing, not for what they were supposed to be doing before altered circumstances intervened.[9]

SO WHAT EXACTLY ARE PERFORMANCE STANDARDS, ANYWAY?

We have been using the phrase "performance standards" liberally since the introduction. So what precisely do we mean by it?

Performance Standards are statements that specify or describe desirable work-related behaviors or job outcomes, and that can be evaluated in some objective manner.

Although ideally *all* performance standards would be expressed in terms of job outcomes or products, following the standard management by objective (MBO) format—to [action verb] [task, object of work or result] [by date, or some other measurable criterion]—in many library jobs it is difficult to identify measurable outcomes that can be reasonably evaluated by a supervisor—or at least, by a supervisor who wants to get something else besides evaluations done!

For example, although you might like to know what percentage of your institution's interlibrary loan transactions are completed using the most cost-effective source for the document, in practice the manager responsible for evaluating the ILL staff almost certainly will never have enough time to determine this on a regular basis (although sampling is always an option if the supervisor feels that a specific measure is crucial to an accurate appraisal of an employee's job performance).

The Good News and the Bad News About Objective Performance Standards

Although most experts seem to agree that objective performance standards for employees are a good thing, the world being what it is, nothing is ever all good or all bad. I will begin with the benefits, but also give you an honest assessment of the drawbacks as well.

First, The Good News

- A complete set of performance standards can be compared against your mission statement to be sure that you are really doing all the things you set out to do.

- Performance standards allow you to call employees to account if they are neglecting certain aspects of their jobs that you think are important, but that they may not. Performance standards are the only way to ensure that all the jobs get done.

- Performance standards can guide you in resetting organizational priorities; examination of priorities may lead you to identify tasks that are no longer needed, or help you spot employees who could, because they are already performing similar functions, take on new responsibilities.

- Performance standards can help to equalize workload distribution—in some cases it may become evident that some people are charged with too much, and some with too little.

- Objective performance standards make you better able to correct the "sinners" and reward the "saints"— especially when a number of people are all engaged in the same or similar tasks, a set of performance standards allows you to compare job performance more equitably.

- Performance standards equally applied help individuals acquire a more realistic picture of their accomplishments. Sometimes the most productive staff members have the lowest self-esteem, and those who are doing the least don't seem to notice that they're not pulling their weight.

- Workers can't improve unless they know specifically where they are falling down on the job; performance standards provide the necessary feedback.

- There are fewer hard feelings when merit raises are given or promotions announced if everyone knows that all are being evaluated systematically and fairly under a consistent system.

- Employees are happier when they feel that they have some input into the standards by which they will be evaluated, and that, in a sense, they are helping set organizational priorities; they feel more like owners of the organization than like mere wage slaves.

- Productivity gains follow when staff have been clearly informed about what is expected of them, and when they know that they will be evaluated accordingly.

- Performance standards based on specific jobs make more sense than vague and inadequate systems that are supposed to apply to everyone, but that can't possibly provide meaningful information.

- Specific performance standards avoid the trap of trying to evaluate people on attitudes or vague qualities (such as "initiative," "enthusiasm," or "creativity") that can never be anything *but* subjective.

- The points assigned to specific standards or groups of standards allow you to communicate to employees the value that the institution places on certain tasks; in other words, the values assigned need not correspond precisely to the amount of time a person usually spends on the task, if in the manager's view, some tasks are more important than others.

And Now the Bad News

As I promised, there are objectionable aspects to objective performance criteria.

- Setting performance standards to place staff members along some sort of evaluative continuum (that determines such things as annual merit increases) can lead to a competitive work environment in which productivity actually decreases.

Time for a reality check: If the rating I get on my annual performance evaluation results in my getting a higher raise than you do, or even something as simple as more favorable treatment by the boss, why should I help you to do your job better?

Answer: Although this attitude can appear (at least covertly) it usually does not occur as long as the new performance appraisal system is not imposed on staff from the top. It should instead be developed in consultation with them after there is clear understanding of what the organization hopes to achieve by creating the system. Managers must be sure that employees are aware of how such a system can actually help *them*, not just the institution. Furthermore, standards can be designed to include criteria that reward teamwork: for example, some measures of group performance could apply across the board to everyone within the work group, so that good performers are actually penalized if they *don't* help those who are less able.

An idealistic view of performance appraisals we often hear is that their only purpose is to rate employees against the goals that they themselves established; however, if the institution really leaves it up to employees to set their own goals, there is no guarantee that the job the institution wants done will really get done. Furthermore, as noted above, appraisals are usually used as a very convenient way to set percentages for annual merit increases.

The ugly truth is that whenever people are placed in a situation in which employees are being compared to each other and compensated differently, the worse your colleagues do, the better you do. You don't have to give into this temptation of course, and we would all like to think that we are above that sort of thing, but the history of humanity proves otherwise. It takes a strong conscience, a very generous spirit, and firm commitment to the institution for an employee to try consistently to bring along weaker staff members if he or she knows that the extra efforts will benefit only the organization, and not the individual.

Here's another problem:

- Employee annual self-evaluations take a lot longer to do under such a system; your part, if you are a manager, takes longer too.

A comprehensive, detailed set of objective performance standards to which employees must respond annually takes serious thought. Some staff members may resent having to devote so much time to a process that was a lot easier before this new-fangled "performance standards" business came along—and they may blame you for giving them more work to do. Furthermore, people know the stakes are high, so they want to do a thorough job and make themselves look as good as possible.

To keep everyone on track, you will need to create and disseminate written guidelines on what is expected, establish and announce annual deadlines, and hold your staff to those deadlines, so that everyone has an equal opportunity to shine. Be prepared for the self-evaluation process to take hours, at least the first time through; eventually you and everyone else (hopefully!) will realize that it was time well spent. The upside is that it definitely goes faster the second time around.

- Creating and maintaining high-quality performance standards is a continuous process: you're never done!

Tip: One way to make the self-evaluation process somewhat less time-consuming is to provide each employee with a copy of his or her standards on a diskette. The standards themselves don't have to be retyped and the staff member can just insert comments into the text that is already there. When the self-evaluation is completed, the staff member can keep a personal copy, and can also copy the entire document, including the self-evaluative remarks, onto a new diskette for the supervisor who can then follow the same process.

Whether we like it or not, jobs are constantly changing, and so must the performance standards used to measure them. Standards will need to be reviewed at least annually, and you may even want your staff to take a look at them every six months or more often, just to be sure the standards still accurately reflect what is expected. Both you as supervisor and the employee should have the power to suggest changes at each "renegotiation" period.

- Setting performance standards still will not cure the problem of supervisors who refuse to supervise, who are uncomfortable with confronting employees, and/or who want to continue giving everyone high ratings whether they deserve them or not.

If your library has one or more such problem people among its managers, before the whole process is over, the department supervisors or some other sort of "equity committee" will have to look at all the performance ratings as a group and equalize them across the whole staff. Meanwhile, the quality of the performance evaluations should definitely be something on which all *supervisors* are rated. After all, while evaluating staff is surely one of the most difficult parts of the supervisor's job, it is nevertheless one of the most important—it is also the main reason they get paid more.

- Concrete, measurable performance standards are very hard to write for jobs that do not yield a product.

Librarianship is only one of many examples of open-ended jobs that in most cases are more "process" than product. Of course you can measure things like the "number of books processed in one hour" or the "average number of reference questions answered per week," but none of these things make any statement about quality, which librarians will agree is usually more important than quantity.

For example, what good does it do if a staff member can shelve 300 books in an hour, but 5 percent of them are shelved incorrectly? A misshelved book can be lost for years. The same thing goes for an item processed incorrectly—for instance, when a spine label is produced that doesn't match the call number in your online catalog. Such mistakes are obvious examples, and ones that can actually be caught if supervisors have the time to check up on their staff. But what about reference questions answered incorrectly? Most librarians engaged in service to the public are far too busy to pay much attention to the quality of their colleagues' work; and users, for whatever reason, may either never realize that they have received incorrect and/or inadequate information, or they may be reluctant to complain if they do.

Some research studies over the past few years have focused on exactly this problem. The results of surreptitious observations of reference librarians in several institutions caused much consternation when reported in the literature because these studies indicated that, in some cases, an embarrassingly large percentage of the questions posed by the researchers were answered incorrectly by the librarians. There is no reason to suppose that the reference librarians who participated in these studies are any better or worse than others.

Furthermore, these studies were carefully designed, highly labor-intensive, and conducted over relatively long periods of time. In real life, supervisors cannot possibly spend that much time observing staff in order to arrive at objective measures of competence. For this reason, in public services we almost always are forced to concentrate on evaluating behavioral characteristics that provide only a partial indication of the success of employee efforts. "Behavioral characteristics" include such things as whether a reference librarian gets out of the chair and accompanies the user to the source to demonstrate how it works, or merely remains comfortably ensconced behind the desk and just points. Although the patron is perhaps no more assured of finding the information wanted one way rather than the other, a fairly safe assumption is that the librarian who cares enough to make sure the patron actually does locate the materials will probably also care enough to see that users actually get what they are looking for. Of course we know that this is not always true, so a variety of indicators will be needed.

TOTAL QUALITY MANAGEMENT

Because librarians are typically concerned more about quality than quantity, the TQM (Total Quality Management) craze that swept through business management circles found quite a few disciples among our ranks.

Although philosophically rooted in the work of American industrial engineer Edward Deming, TQM came back to us via Japan. In the early 1960s, some companies had the idea to convene meetings at which employees had a chance to sit down and talk about the kinds of problems they were having in their jobs, and to brainstorm with the group about possible solutions. The purpose was to improve the quality of whatever product they were manufacturing, and so the term "quality circles" came to be applied to these groups.[10]

When the quality circle technique became a business management fad in the United States, however, it sometimes failed to produce the same wonderful results that it had in Japan, for a variety of reasons. For one thing, many employees of American organizations lacked the kind of institutional dedication typical among the Japanese, so the time spent in quality circle meetings turned into gripe sessions instead of constructive planning for improvement. In other cases, upper management was responsible for the failure: they expected quality circles to solve their problems, while they themselves had no deep commitment to changing organizational culture, a necessary component of TQM.

Deming's ideas are especially appealing to democratically inclined Americans because of his contention that evaluating workers only on the number of items they could produce and how fast they could do it was fundamentally demeaning, not to mention dehumanizing. Such a system is only appropriate for robots, not human beings with brains who are capable of observing what is wrong with a process and suggesting ways to improve quality, efficiency, or productivity—providing they are respected and taken seriously enough by management to be given the opportunity to express their ideas and be listened to.

The foundations of TQM are as follows:

- Statistical or behavioral measures are used to obtain data which is then analyzed in order to solve problems.
- The needs of the customer are paramount.

- The leaders of the organization exemplify and encourage a culture in which quality is highly valued.

360-Degree Performance Appraisals

A hot new trend in management circles is the concept of 360-degree appraisals. Also called multirater, multiperspective, upward, or full-circle feedback,[11] the idea is to get appraisal information on staff from all the various constituencies that depend on an individual's job performance. Although such systems present many problems (such as: How can ratings be kept confidential? How can you ensure reliability when some raters may not have enough information to appraise accurately, but do it anyway? How can you prevent people from taking advantage of an opportunity to merely take revenge on someone they don't personally like?), it is impossible to deny that having more information, rather than less, will surely result in a more accurate picture of performance. In any event, for such a system to work, and in order for the input received to be useful and valid, precise and objective performance standards are essential.

TQM and Performance Standards: Our Future May Depend on Them

Although Deming scorned merit rating, insisting that, among other things, it destroys teamwork and encourages unhealthy rivalries among employees,[12] in today's culture of accountability, performance standards have become an integral part of the TQM structure. Especially in service organizations like libraries (because they do not manufacture a product), objective performance standards are the "people measures" (sometimes statistical, but usually behavioral) that provide managers with the data that show whether customer service and quality effort are really being achieved.

Although I refer to TQM as a fad, I do not believe that it will go away soon. In the present market-driven economy, which has materially altered nearly all sectors of the American work environment, those companies or institutions that do not pay attention to what their customers want and need are doomed. It may come sooner or it may come later, but even libraries will lose their seemingly secure position if they do not start paying a lot more attention to the kinds of services that people really want and need, instead of just what they think people *ought* to want and need. The trend toward enduser searching and the ever-wider availability of resources on the Internet should give all librarians pause to wonder if our beloved profession may not some day disappear if we, as professionals, fail to establish our value to customers much more clearly than we have in the past.

In the new service economy now coming into being in the United States, people are no longer willing to conform to systems that they view as arbitrary or inconvenient—they merely find other sources for what they want. It is in our best interest to ensure that we are not among those who make access to our resources so difficult, frustrating, and time-consuming that people no longer want to take the trouble to use what we have. The only reason the relatively new job of "information broker" has emerged, for example, is that some users wanted more of librarians than they were able or willing to give; a few clever, entrepreneurial librarians observed this, and, voilà, a brand new industry was born.

For this reason, as well as the reasons mentioned previously, it is essential that library administrators challenge their staffs to not only work smarter, doing more with less, but to do it even better than before! Objective performance standards are one of the best ways to make sure that happens.

NOTES

1. E. Eichel, *Performance Appraisal: A Study of Current Techniques* (New York: Research and Information Service, American Management Assn., 1984), 9.

2. Historical facts in this section are taken from F. Lopez, *Evaluating Employee Performance* (Chicago: Public Personnel Assn., 1968), 27–31.

3. Eichel, 7, 11.

4. Information in this entire section is from the *Federal Regulatory Directory*, 6th ed. (Washington, D.C.: Congressional Quarterly, 1990), 108–119.

5. J. Davidson, "Note: The Temptation of Performance Appraisal Abuse in Employment Litigation," *Virginia Law Review* 81 (September 1995): 1605–1606.

6. Information in this section is taken from P. Veglahn, "Key Issues in Performance Appraisal Challenges: Evidence from Court and Arbitration Decisions," *Labor Law Journal* 44 (October 1993): 595–598.

7. Davidson, 1607.

8. Veglahn, 601.

9. This list is partially based on one included in Veglahn, 606.

10. M. Sashkin, *Putting Total Quality Management to Work* (San Francisco: Berrett-Koehler, 1993), 5–11.

11. D. Bracken, "Straight Talk About Multirater Feedback," *Training* 48 (September 1994): 44.

12. M. Barrier, "Who Should Get How Much—and Why?" *Nation's Business* 83 (November 1995): 58.

2. Rewriting or Reforming Your Library's Performance Standards: The Process

Good management technique dictates providing for wide staff involvement in any changes that seriously impact your institution. Particularly when changing performance standards, proceed with caution, because few things you do as a manager will have greater potential for creating negative feelings than the task of transforming a performance evaluation system with which people are comfortable.

The first task is convincing everyone that undertaking such a project is necessary, beneficial, and important. If you are a manager, begin talking about it in staff meetings as a future goal long before you do anything concrete to move the process forward. You may want to introduce certain aspects of it, such as some form of peer evaluation, prior to actually doing anything about specific performance standards of individuals.

The literature provides much encouragement for establishing objective performance standards, even though there is surprisingly little that is of *practical* use. Copy the articles you like and distribute them to others, to start getting people interested in the idea, and bring discussion of these articles into meetings and informal professional conversations. You are likely to find that your best colleagues will be supportive because they too, whether explicitly conscious of it or not, have probably felt hampered by the lack of standards specific enough either to provide genuine guidance to their subordinates, or for themselves as supervisees.

Many librarians who have been promoted into management, no matter how self-confident, find the annual performance appraisal cycle one of the more difficult tasks facing them in their jobs. Let's face it: the majority of us did not enter the profession because we wanted to be "leaders of men" (or more accurately, "of women"!). More likely, we wanted to work with information in its various forms, but because we were good at what we did, we ended up getting promoted, and now we are faced with personnel tasks that we may not particularly relish. And if you're not a supervisor (yet) I would be willing to bet that even *you* don't anticipate with joy the thought of your annual review! It's just human nature not to want to judge or be judged—to tell unpleasant truths, perhaps, to people you like, or worse yet, hear them yourself from the boss.

When you feel that enough time has passed and the climate is receptive, if you are in charge, you may wish to select a committee representative of the diverse constituencies among the library staff: professionals and paraprofessionals, public services and technical services. Each area will contribute a valuable perspective needed in order for the final product to be truly valid and useful. If you decide to go that route (rather than writing the new standards yourself), choose the members from among your most productive and respected employees. These staff members will probably be the ones who are too busy to take on such a project, because they are the loyal staffers who are already wholeheartedly and enthusiastically engaged in the fulfillment of your institutional objectives. Nevertheless, these are exactly the kind of people you need—you probably wish you had more like them! When you ask each of them to serve, remind them why they were chosen, because they deserve to know in advance that they are being entrusted with a delicate and crucial long-range task that may subject them to jealousy, resentment, and criticism from other staff members. And if you are *not* an administrator, go to someone who does have the power to make changes, and volunteer to chair a committee to take a look at your institution's performance criteria; I suspect your offer will be gratefully accepted.

The time commitment involved for such a project will vary depending on the complexity of the institution; I believe, however, that having this book in hand should lift at least some of the burden. With the pressure of having to keep up with their regular jobs, no one is likely to have large amounts of time to devote to this task—even for a medium-sized library, working with staff in a thorough process of developing performance standards from scratch could easily take two years or more.

If you are the person who has convened the committee— as library director, department head, or whatever—when you meet to give the committee its charge, have the courage to give them the freedom to do the job as they best see it. Indicate that you will not interfere with what they do, but that you are available to answer questions or meet with them periodically if they want you to: otherwise, let *them* do it. If the group has been well chosen, you are almost guaranteed to get excellent results, and you have the additional benefit of already having in place a core group of influential staff members who will buy into the new system because they created it themselves. They will also help you "sell it" to the rest of the staff, some of whom may resist the changes at first. And again, if you are not the convener, but a member of the committee, urge your superiors to empower you by giving the group's "creativity quotient" full opportunity for expression; you, after all, are the ones who have the most to lose if the processes and procedures you design are not the best of which you're capable.

THE MODULAR APPROACH TO
PERFORMANCE STANDARDS

One way you can make the task easier is by adopting what I call a "modular approach" to performance standards. Even a few moments of thought about the project before you begin will quickly lead to the recognition that some groups of tasks are common to all employees, others are common to all supervisors, and some are common to all professionals or all paraprofessionals: therefore, any one individual's performance standards could easily be constructed by assembling them from a standardized series of modules, selecting those functional areas that apply to the specific job and leaving out those that do not.

Examples of possible contents of some of these modules is provided in the chapters that follow, but to help make this a little clearer right now, I will use my previous position as an example. My set of performance standards as Coordinator of Off-Campus Library Services included the following modules: (1) Unit/Division/Department Head, (2) Reference Desk Worker, (3) Library Instruction Provider, (4) Departmental Liaison, (5) Off-Campus Services, (6) Service to the Institution, and (7) Academic Achievement. The only one of these that was unique to my job was, of course, Off-Campus Services, because, with the exception of that one area, other people in the library where I work are also engaged in many of the same tasks. Ultimately, the modular approach makes everything much simpler (and inherently more equitable) because everyone who is responsible for fulfilling tasks within a given area is evaluated by exactly the same standards as everyone else.

Obviously, the total *value* placed on any one of those modules can and probably will differ from person to person, however. For instance, although employees with the job title of Reference Librarian will still use the same Reference Desk Worker module as I do, the percentage of total evaluation points devoted to that set of tasks will be considerably more than mine, because that is the major portion of their job—whereas I am only assigned to work on the reference desk two hours per week and one or two weekends per quarter. Therefore, if I get a relatively low score in the category of "Reference Desk Worker" (because I am almost certainly not going to be as proficient at those tasks as are the Reference Librarians who work the desk every day) it will not have a major impact on my total evaluation score because, within the institutional performance standards framework, the time I spend working at the reference desk is not valued as highly as the time I spend performing the tasks delineated in my major responsibility, the Off-Campus Services module. The total percentage of points devoted to any one module is a matter to be negotiated between the individual and the administration, although the committee, since it will rather quickly develop a sense of the needs of the whole library, can probably provide valuable input in that area as well.

If you want to put some aspects of the new system into operation as soon as possible, it probably makes most sense to work on the modules that apply to groups of employees, rather than individuals, so I recommend that you first concentrate on getting those portions of the task out of the way. Besides the advantages enumerated above, adopting this approach also enables the committee to ease into the task: it gets harder from then on!

USING JOB ANALYSIS TO CREATE
PERFORMANCE STANDARDS

Do not be intimidated by the phrase "job analysis." Although there are many books about this subject—most of them very technical—what I have in mind here is simple: whoever is responsible for preparing the new performance standards should request that each staff member submit a list (as complete as possible) of all the various tasks associated with his or her work. Although you probably already know many of these, you may be surprised at what you will learn, both about what is done and what is not done. This process will incidentally give you a certain insight into what the priorities of the individual are, as well as alert you to possible omissions that need to be corrected. Unless you have a well-developed, systematic training program in place for new hires, it is quite likely that to a degree, some employees may have been left to figure out much of their jobs themselves. Setting up a new system of objective performance standards is an ideal way to remind or inform employees about the library's expectations for their positions, because after they have supplied their task lists, you are then free to add whatever duties have been omitted, and, even more importantly, to specify such parameters as the time frame in which these tasks should be completed, and the level of quality expected.

The advantages are obvious: after the new standards have been in place for a year, when the annual performance review under the new system is conducted, the person being evaluated will have to address each item of the standards in his or her self-evaluation, as will the supervisor. At long last, the manager possesses a schematic of specific duties against which job performance can be measured, instead of a series of vague, abstract generalizations which make it all too easy to overlook inadequacies because there is no direct cue to address them. Concentrating on tasks eliminates the temptation to evaluate people on attitudinal factors (such as apparent willingness to do the work, or enthusiasm) and helps to minimize the impact of feelings, personality, and other factors primarily based on emotion rather than facts.

Standard/Above-Standard Performance Criteria

You may feel that you want to try to define both standard and above-standard performance for all tasks. I would recommend against that, because ultimately it is impossible to define above-standard performance in advance. For those employees who are exceptionally creative, intelligent, or highly motivated, you will most likely aim too low if you try to specify what *excellent* performance is—your outstanding workers will probably exceed it. And when they do, is it really fair to keep setting the bar higher and higher, until you finally set a goal so high that they cannot achieve it? This doesn't reward, but instead tends to discourage your best employees, who really are only competing with themselves anyway, not with other staff members. The most you can demand (and, in many cases, realistically expect to get) is standard performance—and unfortunately, even *that* may be beyond some people.

RATING SCALES: WHAT IS "AVERAGE"?

On a scale of 1 to 100, 50 is average. The psychological problem inherent in designating someone as *average* is pretty obvious: during our long years as students, most of us spent a lot of time striving for 100 percent, or at least above 90 percent—an A. When you were a kid, if you ever came home with a grade of 50 percent on a test, you were undoubtedly depressed because you knew you would be in trouble as soon as your mother found out! Despite all the current emphasis on developing self-esteem, it often appears that the real problem now is that we all have plenty of it, maybe even *too much*: none of us considers himself or herself to be average (although of course most of us are), and no one feels good about a score of 50 on anything. On the other hand, using some form of numerical rating scale is about the only way to compare employees against each other, so that, for example, merit money can be equitably distributed.

Here are two possible solutions, and you can probably think of some others:

- Use a numerical rating scale other than 1 to 100, so that the automatic translation to percentages is not so obvious. You could use the typical Likert Scale (1 to 5), for example, and still be able to change those numbers into percentages later if you wished, although there is no real need to do so. The point is, numbers can be averaged, manipulated, and compared easily.

- Use descriptive words for categories: you can equate them to numbers afterward. For example, you could simply revert to the traditional *Unsatisfactory, Needs Improvement, Satisfactory, Above Average*, and *Superior*. When you have gathered all the evaluations together, it is a simple matter to translate *Unsatisfactory* to 1, *Needs Improvement* to 2, and so on. If those words remind you of elementary school, there are many other descriptive phrases that could be chosen, for example: *Superb Performer* (5), *Stands Out from the Pack* (4), *Solid Contributor* (3), *Not Quite There* (2), and *Seriously Deficient* (1). If those seem too value-laden or flippant, consider *Always Exceeds Goals, Often Exceeds Goals, Meets Goals, Sometimes Does Not Meet Goals*, and *Never Meets Goals*. The possibilities are endless: the important thing is that you choose words that supervisors understand and agree on, and that can be used to distinguish clearly among the various levels of job performance.

The purpose of all these ratings is to encourage your staff to rate themselves honestly, and to get supervisors to rate their subordinates objectively too, so any scale that serves to blunt the emotional effect of having to evaluate oneself or others as something below the A or B level is helpful. If you do use a scale of 1 to 100, and if you expect that merely by telling employees that an average score is 50 percent and that therefore they had better have excellent documentation to assign a rating above that, you are probably doomed to failure. True, any system you use will have a midpoint that can be recognized as average, but there's a feeling associated with a rating of 60 percent (which is actually *above average*) that can ruin anybody's morale.

In setting up your self-evaluation procedures, you should definitely consider *not* allowing employees to assign a rating to themselves; instead, they could be required only to provide the information/documentation from which the supervisor can set the measure. The reason for this is that if an employee has given himself or herself a value that the supervisor feels is too high, the evaluator will usually have to argue with the disappointed staff member about the amount by which it has been lowered. It is much easier to deal with a situation in which no expectations of a specific score are created in advance. Thus, a possible source of conflict is avoided.

SELF-EVALUATION AND ASSESSMENT/ DOCUMENTATION OF RATINGS

Use of objective performance criteria involves a whole new mind-set for many employees, and so it may be difficult to get some staff members to address their job criteria specifically enough. Especially in cases of individuals who have been coasting for years, not doing a particularly outstand-

ing job, their self-evaluations may be made up of vague gen-
eralities rather than the precise and succinct examples needed
in order to make an accurate assessment of performance.

To nip this in the bud, rather than just asking an employee
to do a free-form self-evaluation based on standards, you
might want to create a form in which consideration of the
criteria cannot be avoided. If the form includes space for
the supervisor to write comments as well, it can save everyone a lot of time. Using the first section of the criteria developed for a Unit/Department/Division Head as an illustra-
tion, Figure 2.1 shows how this could be handled.

This form, following the recommendation made above,
does not allow employees to rate themselves—that task is
reserved for the supervisor. Very specific phrases are used
to describe performance so that the supervisor must consider the performance criteria in assigning a rating, rather
than his or her feelings about the individual. (The slightly
larger box at the lower right is for assigning a numerical rating after the descriptive phrase has been chosen; it will then
be easy to total the individual's score at the end).

While this type of form only requires the employee to justify a standard or above-standard rating, the number of lines
on the form correspond to the number of criteria, a subtle
hint to address each criterion directly. If this is too subtle, it
can be made explicit in the instructions for filling out the
evaluation forms. This approach helps avoid the problem of
the individuals who may consider themselves generally exceptional because of excellence in one or two areas, even
though they may be just average or below in other job tasks.
The form's "fill-in-the-blanks" approach, not only makes it
less likely that the staff member will indulge in ambiguous
abstractions, it also saves the time of both the rater and the
evaluee—employees who are prone to excess verbiage have
no space in which to write too much, so they are forced to
be concise.

Figure 2.1: Sample Page, Unit/Department/ Division Head Evaluation Form

NAME: _____ EVALUATION YEAR: _____

UNIT/DEPARTMENT/DIVISION HEAD EVALUATION ON PERFORMANCE CRITERIA

I. Supervision and administration of unit/department/division
   A. Planning and assessment
      1. General planning (includes but is not limited to):

> Anticipates needs, problems; recognizes trends
> Keeps informed about issues, services, and innovations related to unit/department/division
> Evaluates/relates these ideas, procedures, or projects to the library/department/division's mission
> Informs staff and administration of ideas, plans, policies, and procedures
> Establishes priorities; develops necessary plans, including staffing needs, for the implementation of these services, innovative ideas, or solutions to problems

Assessment: staff evaluations; supervisor observations and record-keeping

EMPLOYEE: If you feel that you deserve an average or above-average rating on this section, provide specific examples of ways in which you have met or exceeded the criteria listed above during the past year:

(1) _____

(2) _____

(3) _____

(4) _____

(5) _____

Supervisor's remarks:

_____

_____

_____

Supervisor's rating of employee on section I.A.1. *(check one)*:

❏ Exceeds ALL job criteria   ❏ Meets job requirements   ❏ Does not meet expected results
❏ Exceeds in some areas   ❏ Meets some, but not all normal expectations

                                                                    ❏

As discussed in Chapter 1, the more kinds of assessment you can get, the better. Because, as we have already noted, people are usually favorably biased toward themselves, a true picture of performance will, whenever possible, include input from all the constituencies affected by the individual's work. In practice, getting this kind of feedback can be very difficult, and in many cases you will have to depend to a great extent on the assessments provided by the employees themselves.

Nevertheless, as much documentation as possible should be supplied in order to help managers weigh the validity of the self-evaluation. A very helpful approach is to ask staff to submit a portfolio along with their self-evaluations. A portfolio, in this context, is a folder of materials that the employee believes support the claim of having satisfactorily (or extraordinarily) performed his or her duties during the past evaluation period (usually one year). This mode of supplying supporting evidence for a performance review is becoming increasingly popular.

Here is a list of materials that should always be included:

- a copy of the person's current job description
- a copy of the standards and goals for the position
- the individual's candid self-evaluation of his or her own standards, specifically addressing each item listed
- documentation or evidence of work completed, tasks accomplished, or progress toward completion of projects

Some examples of other supporting materials that could be included are

- annual reports
- planning, budget, or policy documents prepared by

the employee or that the employee has helped prepare

- special reports prepared by the employee during the evaluation period
- copies of the employee's publications, papers presented, library guides, handouts, new forms designed
- photographs of work
- certificates or transcripts for courses completed
- unsolicited letters from library users or others, which give evidence of exceptional accomplishments
- peer evaluations, or evaluation forms from programs offered
- programs from conferences or meetings attended
- summarized results of user surveys conducted
- magazine or newspaper clippings highlighting the employee's accomplishments or awards

PEER EVALUATIONS

As mentioned above peer evaluations could be included in the portfolio. Such evaluations are often a touchy subject, since from childhood we have all been indoctrinated against becoming a "tattle-tale." For most children, the worst thing you can be accused of is telling on your friends (although telling on your siblings was okay!).

On the other hand, who knows more about the work of others than those who work with them? Some libraries that have tried peer evaluation found it necessary to limit their use to personal self-improvement, because staff were so resistant to the idea[1]. If you do want to try something formal, Figure 2–2 provides an example of a peer evaluation form deliberately designed to be brief, open-ended, and applicable to all types of library employees.

If you decide to try peer evaluations, the person evalu-

Figure 2.2: Library Staff Peer Evaluation Form

Please respond to the questions below as objectively as possible. If you do not have enough information about the person to make an informed assessment, say so! Do not guess based on what you have heard others say: answer from your own experience. Be professional: do not use this form as an opportunity to vent, but rather, use it to provide constructive feedback that will help your colleague and the library function better.

Name of person being evaluated:

_____

1. Please estimate the number of hours you actually work with or observe this person at work during an average week:

    Work with _____ Observe _____

2. How well does this person interact with patrons and other staff? For example, is he or she courteous and patient? Does he or she convey an attitude of willingness to help? (Circle one.)

N/A	1	2	3	4	5
no opportunity to observe	rude, negative condescending, etc.	barely pleasant	adequate	almost always helpful	amazing!

Please explain, including specific examples if possible: _____

_____

_____

_____

_____

3. Does this person function well as a member of the team? For example, does he or she show up when scheduled, keep you sufficiently informed of his or her plans as they affect your work, follow through with joint projects, share the workload? (Circle one.)

N/A	1	2	3	4	5
no opportunity to observe	this person makes my job harder	needs improvement	acceptable	tries hard	a true colleague

Please explain, including specific examples if possible:

_____
_____
_____
_____

4. Does this person work efficiently, use time well, etc.? (Circle one.)

N/A	1	2	3	4	5
no opportunity to observe	no, wastes time	could improve	acceptable	works hard	extremely productive

Please explain, including specific examples if possible:

_____
_____
_____

5. Does this person seem to possess the knowledge and skills necessary to function effectively in his or her present job? (Circle one.)

N/A	1	2	3	4	5
no opportunity to observe	not qualified	minimally qualified	skills adequate	very qualified	exceptional

Please explain, including specific examples if possible: _____

_____
_____
_____
_____

Additional comments: _____

_____
_____

ated should normally be able to see them, but you might want to consider having them screened first by a highly placed library administrator. Occasionally, an immature or unprofessional staff member with an axe to grind may use the form for revenge. Such cases will be easy to spot, and in my opinion these should be discarded in order to avoid unnecessary and unjustified pain.

Another way to obtain feedback is to solicit spontaneous comments from both peers and library users. You may wish to try using a form similar to that in Figure 2–3. Place blank copies in holders in various locations around the library so that anyone with a gripe or compliment to convey is free to do so. I suggest that the comment forms be deposited in a highly visible locked box near the front door, to which only one or two top administrators have access.[2]

The reason for limited access is that unfortunately you will sometimes need to protect staff members from truly malicious comments. If a form is received unsigned, or is obviously completed by someone wishing to wreak vengeance on a staff member who may have done nothing more awful than enforce library policy, the administrator can weigh the reasonableness of the comment and, if necessary, discreetly discard it before any damage has been done.

You should encourage staff, in addition to the public, to fill out forms. Although the requirement that the comment be signed will usually limit the feedback to positive statements about what someone else has done, it is nevertheless fair that a compliment, when due, be expressed to the person who earned it. Besides the fact that honest and well-deserved praise is one of the best motivators, the feedback form (or a copy of it) can then be passed on to the employee for inclusion in his or her next evaluation portfolio—and any unfavorable ones can be used as the basis for a conference with the supervisor if deemed necessary.

Figure 2.3: Sample Comment Form

WE CARE WHAT YOU THINK ABOUT OUR LIBRARY SERVICES...

If there's something you'd like us to know, please tell us about it:

WHO: _____

WHEN: _____

WHAT: _____

_____

_____

_____

Your name: _____

If you would like someone to contact you regarding your comment, please give us your phone number or e-mail address:

_____

PLEASE DEPOSIT COMMENTS IN THE BOX NEAR THE LIBRARY'S MAIN ENTRANCE. THANKS FOR YOUR CONCERN!

RATING THE RATERS: SUPERVISORS AS EVALUATORS

Ultimately, any performance standards system you establish will only be as good as the managers who actually conduct the evaluations. Many administrators truly dread doing evaluations, because

- they want to avoid conflict
- they fear that their assessment of an employee will be "second-guessed," or will not be supported by their own supervisors
- while they may have confidence in their judgment about an employee, they may lack the facts to back it up
- they may be afraid that if they give a negative but honest assessment, they may get back some equivalent feedback about themselves[3]

If you have supervisors under you who are unable to deal with the confrontational aspects of performance appraisal, or who lack the integrity, honesty, and nerve to at least *try* as best they can to do it objectively, then you have a circumstance that calls for action on your part. Such supervisors may need one-on-one coaching from you, or exposure to some role-playing, or perhaps they could benefit from taking a course on this subject. This is not a situation you can afford to ignore; a large part of a manager's job is to ensure that subordinates get all the help they need in order to perform their own jobs at an acceptable level. Furthermore, it is in your own self-interest to help them, because the problems they cause if they cannot do their jobs will ultimately fall on you.

My view is that this is one of those difficult tasks that fully justify managers' relatively higher salaries, and that if someone in a supervisory position does not or will not recognize and accept this responsibility, then he or she should not hold such a position. The unfortunate reality is that the consequences predicted by the Peter Principle often lead to excellent librarians being promoted into positions for which they have neither the necessary leadership skills nor the requisite courage. Contrary to what many of those who have never actually been "The Boss" may think, being an administrator is all too often primarily rewarding in the monetary sense, and not personally or emotionally rewarding. But the only way to convince some people of this is to let them try it.

Even those supervisors who try to be fair in evaluating employees may still fall prey to what is called "rater error." Such error is the result of human factors, such as inconsistency or personal bias, that unconsciously cause an evaluator to rate an employee inaccurately.[4]

Following are the major types of rater errors identified by researchers, along with their normal consequences:

RATING TOO LENIENTLY. This error occurs when the manager gives staff higher ratings than they deserve and, what is even more problematic, ratings that are clearly much higher than those they would receive from other supervisors in the same library. This is probably the most common rating problem, and there are many possible reasons for it: the desire to be liked by the staff; personal insecurity; the wish to appear to be an effective manager to those above ("all my employees are outstanding, so I must be doing a good job!"); justification for possibly ill-advised hiring decisions; general human reluctance to tell someone the unpleasant truth; and the tendency to rate highly those who are like oneself. The unfortunate consequences can be undeserved promotions and resentment, later on in the staff members' careers, of those supervisors who rate staff more accurately— that is, lower.

RATING TOO HARSHLY. Some supervisors seem to think that they can challenge employees to do better by giving them lower ratings than they deserve. Actually, however, this practice usually lowers morale and can be the motivation for filing a grievance.

CENTRAL TENDENCY. This is the term used to describe those who habitually rate everyone as average or near-average. The supervisor may be a person who is wary of extremes; he or she may feel that there is not enough information to evaluate the employee accurately. The evaluation system itself may subtly push evaluators in this direction if the evaluator is required to supply substantial documentation for scores much above or below the norm; lack of time or energy may simply make it easier to rate everyone as average.

HALO EFFECT. If an employee has a strongly positive or negative personality, the fact that the person is rated at an extreme on one measure can cause the evaluator to unconsciously rate the employee similarly in other areas.

RECENCY. Because our retention of facts from the past is often not as good as we would like, this error is a common problem. If some distinctive event occurs close to the time of the annual evaluation, the supervisor's recollection of it, whether positive or negative, may influence the evaluation unfairly. (This is another reason that regular documentation of employee performance is so important; when evaluating, it is not easy to take into consideration a long period of performance without some notes to jog the memory.)

CONTRAST. If the supervisor has just finished an evaluation of one employee and then turns immediately to another, the judgment of the second can be affected; the supervisor unconsciously compares the second person to the first. This is a well-known psychological phenomenon, whereby review of something very good followed by review of something not as good causes us to exaggerate its bad qualities, and vice versa. Knowing this, supervisors should try as much as possible not to do too many evaluations within a short time period. (Admittedly, sometimes they may have no choice. At least they should try to take a break between appraisals, perhaps to complete other tasks, because time has a significant impact on the strength of contrast rating errors.)

ATTRIBUTION. This error occurs when a supervisor presumes to know the cause—either internal or external—for an employee's positive or negative behavior, and takes that presumed factor into account when rating the person. For example, the evaluator may decide that the staff member's poor performance is a result of laziness or stupidity, characteristics that cannot be changed: viewing the staff member as hopeless, the supervisor does not encourage or even expect the employee to be capable of any improvement.

To help avoid rating errors, involve supervisors in the process of establishing the meaning of any evaluative terms, such as "outstanding," used by all those involved in doing ratings. Especially helpful are the practices discussed in Chapter 1, that is the use of multiple raters and employee self-evaluations; another helpful practice, alluded to above, is the habit of regularly making notes on employee performance whenever something happens that the supervisor will want to recall at appraisal time. Such notes should go beyond merely being filed in the person's folder: giving an employee a written memo either criticizing or praising is the best way to provide the feedback needed for good performance on a regular basis. One of the worst things a supervisor or supervisee can experience is a situation in which a negative performance evaluation comes as a surprise to the employee. Furthermore, workers have a right to know how they are doing more often than once a year.

Because this is such an important part of their jobs, those who are responsible for evaluating others should have a component in their own performance standards in which their effectiveness as evaluators is assessed. When comparing the evaluations of one supervisor with those of another, it will be easy to see who is being the most objective, who is or is not able to confront staff confidently when needed, who takes the time to conduct thorough evaluations, and who gets through the task as quickly as possible, and shortchanges employees in the process. It is a truism of management that the most valuable and expensive resource an organization has is its people. Therefore it is vital that this resource be utilized fully, efficiently, and wisely. High quality, thoughtful, accurate personnel evaluations are one of the most important ways to ensure that this happens.

FOR ACADEMIC LIBRARIANS ONLY

If you are operating in the higher education environment and some or all of the professional library staff have faculty status, you will do well to try to incorporate into your performance standards as many of the requirements specified in your institution's faculty handbook as possible. The advantages of doing this are many. For one thing, the individuals affected will be annually assembling much of the documentation needed for tenure and promotion anyway (or post-tenure review if you have it), so the material can serve double duty. In cases where adequate records have not been kept, it is extremely difficult to go back over many years of employment and develop a full vita from scratch; for fallible humans, this is an easy thing to put off, unless someone is forcing them to do it.

Another benefit is that you can tailor your library's standards for service to the institution, academic achievement, and professional growth to whatever standards have been set by your institution, to ensure that your professionals are being reminded at least annually of those standards, and that they are being required to meet them. Thus, there should be no unpleasant surprises after many years of apparently successful employment. If one of your librarians fails to qualify for tenure and chooses to fight it in court, you may even be legally liable if you have failed to regularly and adequately review each librarian's progress toward tenure or if you have not documented your efforts to systematically inform them of the requirements toward which they should be working.

NOTES

1. Very applicable to this issue is the excellent case study by Diane Schwartz and Dottie Eakin ("Reference Service Standards, Performance Criteria, and Evaluation," *Journal of Academic Librarianship* 12 (March 1986): 4–8) in which they discuss attempts to establish peer evaluation procedures in a medical library. Also relevant are the articles cited in Chapter 5 by Gay Helen Perkins, in which she recounts the problems that a university library worked through to gain acceptance for a special form of peer evaluation, "upward evaluations" (appraisals of supervisors by their subordinates).

2. An interesting case study offered by A. J. Anderson ("Can Store Service Policy Fit a Library?" *Library Journal* 115 (November 1990): 64–66) gets at the pros and cons of the issue of evaluation of library staff by the public.

3. This list is partially based on one contained in Mary Mavis, "Painless Performance Evaluations," *Training* 48 (October 1994): 40.
4. For this discussion of rating errors, I have relied on the excellent summary of research provided by Gary N. Hartzell in "Avoiding Evaluation Errors: Fairness in Appraising Employee Performance," *NASSP Bulletin* 79 (January 1995): 41.

3. Performance Standards for Paraprofessional Staff

- Circulation Assistant
- Library Bookkeeper/Accounting Assistant
- Serials Assistant
- Acquisitions Assistant
- Government Documents Assistant
- Interlibrary Loan Assistant
- Cataloging Assistant
- Off-Campus Services/Extension Assistant
- Reference Assistant
- Shelving Assistant
- *Service to the Institution, Professional Growth and Development

The job criteria included in this chapter are for typical library jobs that exist in many types of libraries. In most cases, these functions are fulfilled by paraprofessionals, but certainly not always. Some of these tasks may be done by student workers or by professionals, depending on the needs and customs of the local library.

It goes without saying that not all of the standards mentioned will apply in every place—and an individual library

---

*mainly for academic libraries, but could apply in any library where such criteria are important

will undoubtedly think of some that need to be added—but most can probably be easily adapted to fit a variety of situations. The goal here is merely to show how the principles of writing objective performance standards can be applied to specific positions, and to give readers guidance as to what sorts of performance standards would probably be included under each position, and how these might be expressed. Where specific numbers are given for measurable objectives, they are included merely as examples; your library will undoubtedly want to think about this and establish what you consider to be reasonable goals for your own situation.

It is expected that these sets of performance criteria could replace standard job descriptions since they go so much further, spelling out precisely what a job entails and the tasks to be accomplished. Because of the complexity of most library jobs today, each grouping actually contains a mixture of measurable standards, qualitative standards, and task descriptions. To evaluate performance adequately, it is crucial that both employee and supervisor regularly document concrete examples that illustrate successful (or unsuccessful) performance as they arise, so that these can be cited in the annual performance review. This, however, does not have to be a formal process—dated notes slipped into a folder, with just enough detail to jog the memory, will do very well!

Note: When using the standards in this chapter (and indeed the standards for all positions included in this book), it will be necessary for the individual library to decide what percentage of the employee's time (and the corresponding weight to be given on the performance evaluation) should be allotted to each function. The group of tasks included in the Circulation Assistant module, for example, could comprise anywhere from 10 percent to 70 percent or more of an individual employee's performance criteria, depending on the needs of the library and the other duties assigned to the specific individual. For example, if the employee only helps out in Circulation during lunch breaks, the weight assigned to Circulation tasks would obviously be light; but if the person is assigned to work in the Circulation Department full-time, then the weight would be far greater. In addition, not all of the tasks defined below would—or could—necessarily be done by one person. The standards below represent a composite of typical Circulation Department tasks.

CIRCULATION ASSISTANT

A. Possesses a working knowledge of all aspects of the library's automated system that pertain to this position. Includes, but is not limited to:

Independently and thoroughly trains new workers to use the system

Makes constructive suggestions for needed system revisions when software upgrades are being considered

Resolves system use problems for less-experienced workers without having to consult others

Takes responsibility for becoming familiar with upgrade changes without prompting from supervisor

Accurately updates and adds records (e.g., user information) to system as required

Assessment: patron/staff feedback, supervisor observations

B. Desk duties
Includes, but is not limited to:

Assumes proactive leadership role during scheduled and assigned desk duty

Supervises routine at desk to accomplish efficient and accurate charging and discharging of all types of materials

Is punctual for desk duty and remains there except for scheduled breaks

Maintains good relations with the public and other library staff; communicates effectively, courteously, and tactfully

Monitors work of subordinates to ensure that such tasks as discharging and preshelving are done correctly

Keeps copiers near desk filled with paper and toner

Performs opening and closing procedures correctly

Dispatches incoming workers to assigned tasks and monitors time spent away from the desk on such activities as picking up and shelving

Deals with patron complaints and problems patiently and decisively

Assists library users in locating materials or refers them appropriately to others who can help

Checks applications for borrower's cards for completeness and processes them according to established library procedures

Assessment: all materials returned during shift have been discharged and preshelved before the assistant finishes his/her desk duty period; patron/staff feedback; supervisor observations

C.   Personnel supervision
Includes, but is not limited to:

Assists with training of new workers, resulting in competent new employees

Assists with scheduling of assistants and keeping them on task

Helps to find replacements when absences occur

Maintains appropriate level of authority with subordinates

Assists in evaluation process by documenting job performance of subordinates for the Circulation Department Supervisor

Models good work habits for others (i.e., avoids personal phone calls while on duty, stays on task, etc.)

Corrects subordinates courteously but firmly when required

Assessment: supervisor observations, peer and patron feedback

D. Stack/file maintenance
   Includes, but is not limited to:

Checks assigned portion of library collection daily in order to identify problem areas
   • makes recommendations for materials to be sent to storage
   • assigns shelf-reading and straightening to shelvers
   • checks shelves to see that materials are in good order
   • notices areas requiring shifting and assigns projects to shelvers
   • assigns shelvers the task of moving of materials to storage
   • ensures that assigned areas always appear neat and orderly
   • keeps supervisor informed of collection management plans

Keeps collection records up to date
   • at intervals specified by library policies, schedules and runs reports for items that are long overdue
   • conducts extensive search in stacks for long-overdue items
   • discharges items found, submits reorder forms for missing items to Acquisitions for review
   • changes item location in online catalog to indicate status (e.g., lost, missing, etc.)
   • enters data into spreadsheets for annual periodicals use tracking

Assessment: supervisor observations, peer and patron feedback

E. Overdue/delinquent process
    Includes, but is not limited to:

    Schedules charge list report to run at designated times

    Within two days completes checking list against stacks
    and pulls, discharges, cancels fines for any items found
    on shelves

    Schedules and runs delinquent user report and promptly
    sees that these users are blocked/barred in the system

    Oversees running delinquent notices for overdue items
    and bills

    Mails overdue notices to patrons the day after shelves
    checked

    Assessment: supervisor observations, peer feedback

F. Searches and holds
    Includes, but is not limited to:

    Conducts daily searches for missing items or other ma-
    terials requested by patrons

    Notifies patrons of items found on the same day that
    materials are located

    If item is to be sent to a branch location, checks item
    out and places it in the courier container on the same
    day that it was pulled from shelves

    Submits reorder request to Acquisitions for items miss-
    ing 90 days or more

    *Assessment: supervisor checks search-and-hold files
    weekly; patron/staff feedback; search success rate statis-
    tics*

G. Other departmental tasks
    May include:

Statistics
- maintains up-to-date records of use as prescribed by supervisor
- files and keeps statistics in good order, readily available as needed
- submits accurate reports by specified deadline dates
- keeps Department Head informed about collection use and any problems encountered in collecting statistics

Assessment: peer feedback, portfolio, self-evaluation, supervisor observations

Equipment maintenance
- assists Systems Librarian in maintaining and cleaning departmental computers, barcode wands, printers, etc.
- daily cleans microfilm equipment, photocopiers, and any other assigned equipment

Assessment: feedback from Systems Librarian, patrons, staff; supervisor observations

Personnel backup
- assists in performing essential duties of absent staff members without prompting from supervisor
- offers to help at Circulation Desk whenever assigned staff appear overwhelmed

Assessment: peer feedback, supervisor observations

Processing of reserve materials (academic libraries)
- promptly pulls books from collection as requested on reserve lists received from faculty so that materials can be ready for use within 48 hours of request

- changes item locations in automated system (e.g., from STACKS to RESERVES)
- revises circulation period according to faculty request
- prepares photocopies for circulation by placing them into clearly labeled folders and Princeton files, or scans reserve materials and loads them into electronic reserve system
- knows and follows copyright guidelines regarding reserve materials
- enters reserve list into automated system under faculty name and course

Assessment: faculty/student/peer feedback; supervisor observations

Time cards/annual and sick leave records, etc.
- maintains calendar on which departmental staff record annual and sick leave in easily accessible, specified location
- checks time cards and accurately computes leave
- summarizes and reports leave time as required
- checks part-time worker time cards, computes hours
- prepares cards for supervisor's signature by specified date/time

Assessment: supervisor observations; staff, Payroll Clerk/ Dept. feedback

Signage
- makes and posts attractive and accurate shelf range labels and signs providing information on changes in library hours and holidays
- promptly removes signs that are outdated or no longer needed

Assessment: supervisor observations, staff/peer/patron feedback

Lost and found

- records found items in logbook
- places valuable items in secure location
- handles unclaimed items according to library policies and procedures at the end of each week
- records in log the disposition of unclaimed items

Assessment: supervisor observations, staff/peer/patron feedback, portfolio

Materials repair

- neatly stores books or other items needing repair until repair work is completed
- orders necessary supplies in advance so that they are available when needed
- ensures that repairs are done competently and promptly
- checks out in system those items in need of repair or rebinding so that they can be accounted for
- promptly sends severely damaged materials to Bindery Clerk for evaluation

Assessment: supervisor observations, staff/peer/patron feedback

LIBRARY BOOKKEEPER/ACCOUNTING ASSISTANT

A. Efficiently supervises expenditure of funds
    Includes, but is not limited to:

    Records library purchases/transactions in ledger or computer spreadsheet daily/weekly

    Maintains financial records of all library funds

    Updates records within 3 days of receipt of invoices/purchase orders

    Audits transactions records by comparing with Business Office printout within 5 days of receiving printout

    Notifies Business Office of any errors found within 48 hours

    Posts payments in library's online system within one working day

    Prepares financial/budget summary for submission to supervisor by 15th day of each month

    Prepares purchase orders for equipment/supplies within 2 days of receiving specifications

    Obtains comparative bids within 3 working days whenever needed

    Receives checks for disbursement to vendors, records check numbers in register, and prepares checks and invoices for mailing within 1 business day

    Audits vendor statements/invoices, requests clarifications as necessary, and resolves discrepancies within 4 business days

    Maintains accurate and organized filing system (filing done daily)

    Prepares bills/account fund transfers for charge-backs (e.g., to academic departments)

Provides estimates of annual expenditures in various categories as requested, for preparation of library budget (within one week of request)

At direction of supervisor, prepares and submits budget amendments to transfer funds from one account to another

B.   Handles all money receipts and cash
     Includes, but is not limited to:

Checks cash available in Circulation money drawer at least 2 times per day and replenishes change as necessary

Before leaving each Friday, ensures that sufficient cash is available in Circulation Dept. safe to cover weekend needs

Checks bill changer/vendacard dispenser/library vending machines before leaving each day and loads with change

Removes money from copiers daily

Counts and rolls coins, records amounts and copier meter readings

Runs daily cash reports in system and reconciles Circulation cash drawer within 2 hours of opening

Records check numbers for payments received, prepares daily/weekly deposits with no errors, and delivers to bank/Business Office

Handles petty cash reimbursements, stamps, etc.

C.   Provides all other types of accounting support required
     Travel
       • checks travel authorizations submitted by employees to verify for administrators that sufficient funds are available

- updates travel budget summary as funds are expended
- checks for accuracy and completeness, then forwards staff travel claims to the Business Office

Staff account book purchases

- places orders within 5 days
- follows up on back orders monthly
- processes jobber invoices within 2 business days
- notifies staff of receipt of orders within 1 business day
- collects money from staff who have ordered books within 1 week

Personnel

- monitors budget weekly to ensure that funds are being spent at an appropriate rate
- notifies departments promptly if overspending is occurring, to avoid budget shortfalls
- distributes paychecks according to established library procedures

Supplies and photocopying equipment

- checks supply cabinet for standard items weekly and places orders as needed
- processes "special order" supplies requests within 3 days
- evaluates copy equipment by attending vendor demos, etc.
- obtains competitive bids from copier equipment and supplies vendors annually
- checks machines (including supply storage) twice a week

- troubleshoots machines and/or phones copy repair-person within 1 hour of discovering problem
- orders paper, toner cartridges, etc., quarterly or more often as necessary

Assessment: peer/vendor/Business Office feedback, supervisor observations, portfolio items

SERIALS ASSISTANT

A. Possesses a working knowledge of all aspects of the library's automated system that pertain to this position. Includes, but is not limited to:

Independently and thoroughly trains new workers to use the system

Makes constructive suggestions for needed system revisions when software upgrades are being considered

Resolves system use problems for less-experienced workers without having to consult others

Takes responsibility for becoming familiar with upgrade changes without prompting from supervisor

Assessment: patron/staff feedback, supervisor observations

B. Efficiently supervises ordering/processing of new materials received
Includes, but is not limited to:

Telephones or faxes orders for new periodicals/serials to jobber every two weeks

Unpacks boxes received and checks contents against packing slips daily

Accurately (no errors) checks in new periodicals/serials/microforms within 2 days of receipt

Prints shelving labels and applies to items daily

Transfers materials to Circulation for shelving/filing within 2 days of receipt

Types and proofreads correspondence (no errors) related to claims, items missing from shipments, duplicate/exchange, etc., on a weekly basis

Accurately tabulates statistics on new items added to collection and provides reports as scheduled

Checks and verifies invoices for payment same day as received

Maintains accurate and organized filing system (filing done daily)

Assessment: peer/vendor/patron feedback, supervisor observations

C.   Handles maintenance of existing collection
     Includes, but is not limited to:

Pulls periodicals from shelves according to schedule, collates volumes, checks for completeness

Checks previous volume to verify binding instructions, types forms, and packs materials for shipping/pickup

Updates location codes in online system (e.g., for materials sent to bindery, periodicals moved from current to backfiles)

Checks shipments received from bindery within 3 working days of receipt; if necessary, contacts bindery for corrections within one week

Prepares duplicate/exchange lists monthly

Initiates ILL requests for missing/torn out pages within one week of receiving damaged/incomplete items

Tips in missing pages and returns item to shelving area within one week of receiving pages

Prepares orders for periodical backfiles within one day of receiving request from Serials/Acquisitions Librarian

Assessment: peer/vendor/patron feedback, supervisor observations

D. Other duties
    Includes, but is not limited to:

Sends update reports to regional database maintainers every two weeks

Answers telephone promptly (within 4 rings) and courteously

Responds immediately to information requests from public services desks

Arranges for scheduled printouts of periodicals holdings lists in quantities needed; distributes printouts to public services desks

Assists with training of new workers, resulting in competent new employees

Assists with scheduling of subordinates and keeping them on task

Assists in performing essential duties of absent staff members without prompting from supervisor

Assists in evaluation process by documenting job performance of subordinates for the Acquisitions/Serials Department Librarian

Models good work habits for others (i.e., avoids personal phone calls while on duty, stays on task, etc.)

Corrects subordinates courteously but firmly when required

Promptly supplies reports needed for budget planning whenever requested

Assessment: peer feedback, supervisor observations

ACQUISITIONS ASSISTANT

A. Possesses a working knowledge of all aspects of the library's automated system which pertain to this position.
Includes, but is not limited to:

Independently and thoroughly trains new workers to use the system

Makes constructive suggestions for needed system revisions when software upgrades are being considered

Resolves system use problems for less-experienced workers without having to consult others

Takes responsibility for becoming familiar with upgrade changes without prompting from supervisor

Assessment: patron/staff feedback, supervisor observations

B. Efficiently processes orders for new materials
Includes, but is not limited to:

Searches library's online system in order to determine if item ordered is already held (1 error or less per 100 items searched)

Locates correct bibliographic information for items new to system in BIP, OCLC, or other relevant databases (1 error or less per 100 items searched)

Creates new orders in system and sends to vendors (maximum 1 typing error per 10 orders)

Changes order status to received and creates invoice record in online system within 1 business day of receipt (no errors)

Processes standing order arrivals, updates prices in system, and pays invoices within 2 business days

Updates standing order list quarterly (no errors)

Unpacks boxes and checks contents against packing slips, marks date received

Assessment: peer/bookkeeper feedback, supervisor observations

C. Handles invoicing processes promptly and correctly
Includes, but is not limited to:

Prepares invoices daily

Has invoices from the week ready for signature of Acquisitions Librarian and forwarding to Business Office every Friday before noon

Prepares interlibrary loan invoices and sends them to Business Office within 3 business days

Assessment: peer/bookkeeper/Business Office/vendor feedback, supervisor observations

D. Takes responsibility for dealing with donated materials
Includes, but is not limited to:

Searches library's online system weekly to determine if items received are duplicates

Forwards items to Acquisitions Librarian/Collection Development Office, along with copies of system records if available, for decision on disposition

Enters into system those items to be added; forwards items to Cataloging weekly

Prepares gift acknowledgement letters for Director's signature within 2 weeks of receipt of gift

As scheduled, sends to Development/Foundation Office monthly report of gifts received (no errors)

Disposes of duplicates or rejected items within one month, according to library policies and procedures

Assessment: feedback from Acquisitions Librarian, Director, donors, Development Office

E. Other departmental duties
Includes, but is not limited to:

Maintains accurate annual leave/sick leave records for department; has weekly report ready for supervisor's signature by noon on Friday

Answers phones courteously and promptly by 4th ring

Responds to requests from public services desks immediately

Empties 1st class mail basket and readies mail for pickup by mail carrier/Campus Mail driver as scheduled

Types correspondence as needed (e.g., notifications of funds allocations, letters to publishers) accurately and neatly (no errors)

Assists with training of new workers, resulting in competent new employees

Assists with scheduling of subordinates and keeping them on task

Assists in performing essential duties of absent staff members without prompting from Supervisor

Assists in evaluation process by documenting job performance of subordinates for the Acquisitions Librarian

Models good work habits for others (i.e., avoids personal phone calls while on duty, stays on task, etc.)

Corrects subordinates courteously but firmly when required

Maintains accurate and organized filing system (filing done daily)

Promptly supplies reports needed for budget planning whenever requested

Assessment: peer feedback, supervisor observations

GOVERNMENT DOCUMENTS ASSISTANT

A.   Possesses a working knowledge of all aspects of the library's automated system that pertain to this position. Includes, but is not limited to:

Independently and thoroughly trains new workers to use the system

Makes constructive suggestions for needed system revisions when software upgrades are being considered

Resolves system use problems for less-experienced workers without having to consult others

Takes responsibility for becoming familiar with upgrade changes without prompting from supervisor

Assessment: patron/staff feedback, supervisor observations

B.   Efficiently supervises processing of new documents received
Includes, but is not limited to:

Unpacks boxes received and disposes of cartons daily

Checks contents of shipments against shipping lists within 5 working days

Files claims (if needed) for missing items weekly

Stamps date received, depository number, library ownership, etc., within 5 working days

Accurately records SuDocs number on piece in designated location

Informs Documents Librarian of problems/changes in shipments/shipping lists and takes action as directed within 5 working days

Accurately (no errors) adds new documents to check-in/shelflist record within 5 days of receipt

Places small, easily lost documents that have been designated for cataloging into pamphlet binders

Records documents to be cataloged and forwards them to Cataloging Department within 8 working days

Forwards periodicals that will be shelved in general collection to Serials Department on the same day they are checked in

Resolves call number/title problems for Cataloging within 5 working days of request for assistance

Enters data for new documents not being cataloged into online system/shelflist within 10 days of receipt

Prints out shelving labels and applies to items within 2 days of entry

Accurately tabulates statistics on new items added to collection and provides reports as scheduled

Assessment: peer/Cataloging/patron feedback, supervisor observations

C. Maintains collection and assists users
    Includes, but is not limited to:

Maintains accurate and organized filing systems (filing done daily)

Pulls superseded items from shelves and processes according to established policies

Brings items requiring binding to the attention of Documents Librarian

Makes necessary corrections to pieces and holdings records (i.e., as outlined in *Technical Supplement to Administrative Notes*) before next issue is received

Shelves/supervises shelving of documents (98% accuracy)

Shifts/supervises shifting of collection as necessary

Conducts accurate inventory projects as required

Performs minor repairs/relabeling of documents

Creates and maintains accurate signage to aid users in locating documents

Promptly and courteously answers telephone (within 4 rings)

Responds immediately to requests for help from public services desks (e.g., location of items, received status, etc.)

Assessment: peer/patron feedback, supervisor observations

D. Other duties
    Includes, but is not limited to:

Assists with training of new workers, resulting in competent new employees

Assists in performing essential duties of absent staff members without prompting from supervisor

Assists in evaluation process by documenting job performance of subordinates for the Government Documents Librarian

Models good work habits for others (i.e., avoids personal phone calls while on duty, stays on task, etc.)

Assists with scheduling of subordinates and keeping them on task

Corrects subordinates courteously but firmly when required

Supplies Documents Librarian with needed reports within 1 day of request

Types correspondence as needed with no errors

Orders supplies as needed (necessary items are always available)

Assessment: peer feedback, supervisor observations

INTERLIBRARY LOAN ASSISTANT

A.   Handles details of the lending process
     Includes, but is not limited to:

     Pulls requested materials from shelves with 98% accu-
     racy (or, oversees pulling of materials from shelves and
     checks to see that correct item has been retrieved)

     Updates requests on ILL system (e.g., OCLC) daily, to
     indicate that requests will or will not be filled

     Quality checks all materials to be sent to requesting li-
     braries
     • ensures that photocopies are clear and very read-
       able, no pages are missing, etc.
     • flips through books to be sure pages have not been
       torn out, etc.

     Accurately mails or faxes all materials retrieved within
     2 business days (or, oversees delivery of requested ma-
     terials, ensuring that they are sent within 2 business
     days)

     Competently uses the library's online system to charge
     and discharge materials loaned to other libraries

     Keeps track of items that become overdue and sends
     overdue notice as soon as an item is one day overdue

     Processes Special Message File daily

B.   Handles details of the borrowing process
     Includes, but is not limited to:

     Knows how to use the indexes/databases available in
     order to verify citations quickly and accurately

     Takes responsibility for keeping current on changes, up-
     dates, etc., in ILL system, and applies this knowledge
     to the job

Efficiently searches ILL borrowing system to locate libraries that own requested material

Accurately enters requests into the system and selects libraries from which to borrow in accordance with ILL Department policies, regional agreements, instructions from ILL Librarian, etc.

Checks incoming materials before notifying patron that an ILL request has arrived, to be sure that correct item has been sent, no pages are missing from articles, etc.

Updates ILL system daily, to indicate items that have been received

Always informs users of any restrictions on use when item is picked up

Contacts borrowers same day item becomes overdue to request immediate return

Promptly sends renewal requests on ILL system in response to user requests, and notifies users ASAP if extensions have been granted

Checks for e-mail requests daily and processes Special Message File

C. Other departmental duties
   Includes, but is not limited to:

Checks invoices (to be paid/to be sent) for accuracy and forwards to bookkeeper once a week

Keeps accurate records according to library/departmental specifications

Prepares and submits monthly statistics report by 10th of each month

Maintains accurate statistics (for copyright records, etc.)

Types correspondence as needed with no errors

Orders supplies as needed (necessary items are always available)

Makes sure that Reference Desk always has an adequate supply of ILL request forms

Assists with training of new workers, resulting in competent new employees

Assists in performing essential duties of absent staff members without prompting from supervisor

Promptly and courteously answers telephone (within 4 rings)

Models good work habits for others (i.e., avoids personal phone calls while on duty, stays on task, etc.)

Corrects subordinates courteously but firmly when required

Assessment: feedback from peers, patrons, other libraries; supervisor observations

CATALOGING ASSISTANT

A.   Cataloging

Includes, but is not limited to:

Is a competent user of all modules of the library's automated system needed in this position

- correctly edits item records and connects to MARC record
- correctly creates copies, volumes, item records
- runs reports daily and prints labels

Creates new records/workforms with less than 5% error rate

Requires little assistance in completing copy cataloging of assigned materials using national cataloging system (e.g., OCLC) bibliographic records (less than 5% error rate)

- selects correct cataloging system record and edits CIP record to match item in hand
- uses correct ISBD punctuation, AACR2, MARC formats, local authority file, holdings codes, etc.
- exports records correctly
- processes books correctly (labels neat, accurate, and legible)

Takes responsibility for keeping up to date on changes in cataloging codes and formats

Works efficiently, is able to complete assigned work on an average of x items per month

Works cooperatively with departmental colleagues, Acquisitions, and public service areas so that materials flow smoothly and rapidly through the system to the shelves

Keeps accurate statistics as required by supervisor

B. Database maintenance
    Includes, but is not limited to:

    Deals with error reports within one business day

    Edits records for subject heading changes as directed by supervisor within 2 business days

    Files/checks and corrects filing in shelflist, applying knowledge of correct ALA filing rules

    Notices and corrects holdings and other errors in bibliographic databases

    Adds copies/volumes promptly and correctly

    Promptly and correctly processes withdrawals
    - correctly deletes holdings in shared databases (e.g., OCLC, other regional cooperative systems, etc.)
    - correctly edits or removes record in library's online system
    - pulls shelflist cards

    Assessment: peer, user feedback; supervisor observations and sample checking of work; portfolio items; self-evaluation

C. Materials processing
    Includes, but is not limited to:

    Places labels on new or rebound materials neatly and accurately, according to library's established specifications (straight, clean)

    Covers labels with label protectors (straight, no wrinkles)

    Secures date due slips in books (or other materials) according to established specifications (straight)

    Stamps materials with appropriate ownership stamps in locations specified (stamped information clearly readable)

Correctly inserts magnetic detection strips into materials that are to be stripped

When processing is completed, arranges new books on New Books shelves according to class number (or other established procedure)

Files shelflist cards correctly (less than 1% error rate)

Processes reclassified items

- carefully removes old label so as not to damage material
- places new labels on materials neatly and accurately

Processes withdrawals

- stamps DISCARDED in all specified places on the item
- disposes of items correctly, according to library policies and procedures

D. Other departmental duties
   Includes, but is not limited to:

Maintains accurate annual leave/sick leave records for department; has weekly report ready for supervisor's signature by noon on Friday

Answers phones courteously and promptly by 4th ring

Responds to requests from public services desks immediately

Assists with training of new workers, resulting in competent new employees

Assists with scheduling of subordinates and keeping them on task

Assists in performing essential duties of absent staff members without prompting from supervisor

Assists in evaluation process by documenting job performance of subordinates for the Head of Cataloging

Models good work habits for others (i.e., avoids personal phone calls while on duty, stays on task, etc.)

Corrects subordinates courteously but firmly when required

Assessment: peer feedback, supervisor observations

OFF-CAMPUS SERVICES/EXTENSION ASSISTANT

A. Supplies materials in response to student requests
    Includes, but is not limited to:

    On a daily basis, logs requests as they are received and
    stamps with date received

    Logs on to e-mail system and checks for requests at the
    beginning of each day

    On a daily basis puts requests that require searches into
    Coordinator's box for evaluation

    Successfully performs database searches for relatively
    simple topics, as assigned by Coordinator

    Accurately checks library holdings for materials that are
    to be sent and marks lists clearly so that student work-
    ers can retrieve/copy needed items

    When the library does not own a sufficient quantity of
    items identified by the database search(es) and the dead-
    line for receiving materials is at least 10 days in the fu-
    ture, places ILL requests for other relevant materials
    within 1 business day

    If the library does not own a sufficient quantity of ma-
    terials identified in the database search(es) and there is
    not enough time for ILL, checks regional holdings lists
    and advises students of libraries where they could ob-
    tain needed materials within 3 business days

    Quality checks all materials prior to mailing (photocopies
    are clear and very readable, no pages are missing, cor-
    rect item is being sent, etc.) within 1 business day after
    all materials needed for a specific request have been
    assembled

    Prepares accurate invoices and bills student on library
    online system same day materials are shipped

Packs items securely for shipping, prepares clear and correct address label

B.   Supervision of student workers
     Includes, but is not limited to:

Effectively trains new student assistants so that they are quickly able to be productive workers

Is able to resolve almost all student problems

Records errors found during quality checking and either discusses problem with student or refers matter to Coordinator of Off-Campus Services

Provides feedback for quarterly evaluation of student workers

Ensures that all student workers are on task and working efficiently while on duty (helps arrange/schedule tasks, monitors student productivity, etc.)

Keeps Coordinator informed of any problems with student workers

Checks time cards for accuracy and signs them at the end of each pay period

C.   Off-Campus publicity materials, mailings, etc.
     Includes, but is not limited to

Designs attractive and informative flyers, brochures, etc., using word processing software and/or other available desktop publishing software

Secures 3 copies of next quarter's class schedule for the OCS office as soon as this is published

Takes responsibility for seeing that the off-campus faculty database is accurately and completely updated prior to each quarter; prints mailing labels

Sees that needed quantities of forms for quarterly mailing are available at least 2 weeks prior to the next quarter, so that information packets for off-campus faculty can be sent out in a timely manner

Prepares information packets or supervises preparation of packets; all items that need to be sent are included in every packet

D. Prepares materials for off-campus reserve collections
Includes, but is not limited to:

Pulls materials from collection as requested on reserve lists received from faculty within 48 hours of receipt of list

Notifies Coordinator immediately if any items are requested that library does not own

Changes item locations in automated system (e.g., from STACKS to correct reserve location)

Prepares photocopies for circulation by typing cards for manual circulation, placing articles into clearly labeled folders and Princeton files, or scans reserve materials and loads them into electronic reserve system

Knows and follows copyright guidelines regarding reserve materials

Packs materials for shipping to off-campus location

Sends copy of reserve list with specific information on location, contact person at off-campus site, hours open, etc., to the faculty member who requested the reserves

Files original copy of reserve list in Off-Campus Reserve notebook

At end of quarter, arranges for return of reserve materials to main library

When materials are returned, checks to see that all items have been returned, discharges if necessary, and returns items to Circulation for reshelving

E.   Regional cooperative borrowing system
     Includes, but is not limited to:

On a daily basis, stamps cooperative borrowing system card request lists with date received

Checks requests for cooperative borrowing system cards against library and/or registrar's lists to be sure students are registered

Supervises preparation of cards by student assistants

When cards are ready, quality checks cards, photocopies list, and packs cards and list for delivery to class, noting on list the date cards were sent

Files original copy of request list in notebook

F.   Other departmental duties
     Includes, but is not limited to:

Delivers materials to off-campus sites weekly

Models good work habits for others (i.e., avoids personal phone calls while on duty, stays on task, etc.)

Orders/obtains supplies as needed (necessary items are always available in the Off-Campus Library Services office)

Checks answering machine for messages at the beginning of each day, and whenever the office has been empty for at least one-half hour

Forwards phone calls to voice mail whenever leaving the office for more than 10 minutes

Promptly and courteously answers telephone (within 4 rings)

Assessment: portfolio items, feedback from peers/cooperating libraries, self-evaluation, supervisor's observations

REFERENCE ASSISTANT

A. Services equipment in Reference area
    Includes, but is not limited to:

    Ensures that adequate supplies of copier/printer paper are always available in the Reference storage area

    Checks paper supply in copiers and printers at beginning of each day and keeps copiers (including microform) and printers filled with paper until end of shift

    Troubleshoots copy and printing equipment as soon as the need arises (clears paper jams, changes toner cartridges, etc.)

    Cleans LAN workstations, OPAC terminals, and microform machines weekly

B. Provides service to library users
    Includes, but is not limited to:

    Able to assist patrons with simple e-mail and directional questions

    Picks up and accurately shelves reference books at least once every hour so that they are available ASAP for next user

    Assists patrons in use of microform machines and photocopiers (loading film/fiche, how to print, reducing/enlarging, etc.)

    Assists patrons in use of library's online catalog system; is usually able to find materials wanted and helps user locate the materials within the library

    Gives clear and accurate directions to various parts of the library, location of collections, etc.

    Retrieves items from storage at request of librarian or patron

Helps patrons with purchase and revaluing of venda-cards for copiers

Answers phone when a Reference Librarian is not available; transfers calls, takes accurate messages and ensures that messages are delivered as soon as possible

Helps users with simple LAN questions (e.g., how to print and log to disk, reset locked-up workstations, etc.)

C. Other departmental duties
    Includes, but is not limited to:

Keeps accurate statistics according to established library policies and procedures

Reads shelves in Reference at least once every two weeks and performs stack maintenance as needed (e.g., shifting, dusting, etc.)

If Reference workload level permits, may assist other departments by performing tasks that can be done while monitoring Reference area (e.g., making photocopies, applying labels, stamping, etc.)

Assessment: feedback from patrons and Reference Librarians

SHELVING ASSISTANT

A.   Maintains assigned area of library
     Includes, but is not limited to:

As scheduled (e.g. hourly, twice a day), walks through area and picks up materials that have been left on tables, copiers, floors, etc.

Returns materials to sorting area after each pickup

Reports areas needing building maintenance attention (e.g., lights out, furniture broken) according to established library procedures

Takes responsibility for helping to enforce library policies regarding food and drink, noise, etc., during pickup

B.   Maintains assigned stack area in good order
     Includes, but is not limited to:

Correctly reshelves books in assigned area at a minimum rate of 2 books per minute with 98% accuracy[1]

Removes extraneous items left on shelves by users (e.g., paper, lost personal items, etc.) and deals with these items appropriately

Is alert to the existence of misshelved books while shelving, removes and reshelves single items correctly the same day they are discovered

If larger sections are out of order, makes written note of their location and returns to straighten them out within 2 business days

Notices and removes materials in need of repair and takes them to the appropriate department at the end of each shift

Reads 2 sections of shelves weekly

Shifts materials in assigned stack area as needed (ensures that space for reshelving materials is always available)

Dusts shelves and materials according to established schedule

Assessment: observations/measurements by stack supervisor; staff and patron feedback; self-evaluation

SERVICE TO THE INSTITUTION, PROFESSIONAL GROWTH AND DEVELOPMENT

The following standards are primarily for academic libraries, but they could apply in any library where such criteria are important.

Service to the Institution

A. Responds positively and in a timely manner to reasonable requests for assistance from other departments

B. Demonstrates initiative in accomplishing interdepartmental/library goals, and in helping others to accomplish these goals

C. Regularly attends and makes demonstrable contributions to committees whenever appointed

D. Knows and follows system and departmental policies and procedures

    Assessment: supervisor observations, staff feedback, self-evaluation, portfolio items (e.g., copies of committee minutes, etc.)

Professional Growth and Development

A. Takes initiative for informal, self-education in library issues related to the job through reading, attendance at available conferences/seminars/workshops, etc.

B. Engages in formal study designed to upgrade skills and knowledge needed in order to perform at a higher level

    Assessment: portfolio items (e.g., certificates, copies of diplomas, etc.), self-evaluation, supervisor observations

NOTE

1. This tested target figure was given to me by Marc Davis, Manager/ Building Services, University of Nebraska at Omaha Libraries. He has a very well-developed system of shelver accountability which he was kind enough to share with me in response to a listserv query.

4.   Performance Standards for Professional Staff

- Unit/Department/Division Head
- Reference Librarian
- Library/Bibliographic Instruction Coordinator
- Library/Bibliographic Instruction Provider
- Special Collections Librarian/Archivist
- Acquisitions/Serials/Collection Development Librarian
- Cataloger
- Government Documents Librarian
- Circulation Librarian
- Interlibrary Loan Librarian
- Systems Librarian
- Extension/Off-Campus Services Librarian
- Branch Librarian (Public Library)
- Children's/Young Adult Librarian (Public Library)
- Library Media Specialist
- Library Webmaster
- Academic Achievement, Professional Growth and Development, Service to the Institution (Academic Library)

The job criteria included in this chapter are for typical library jobs that exist in many types of libraries. In most cases, these functions are fulfilled by degreed librarians, but certainly not always. Some of these tasks may well be done by paraprofessionals, depending on the needs and customs of the local library.

As in the previous chapter, not all of the standards mentioned here will apply in every place—and an individual library will undoubtedly think of some standards that need to be added—but most can probably be easily adapted to fit a variety of situations. The goal here is merely to show how the principles of writing objective performance standards can be applied to specific positions, and to give readers guidance as to what sorts of performance standards would probably be included under each position, and how these might be expressed. Where specific numbers are given for measurable objectives, they are included merely as examples; your library will undoubtedly want to think about this and establish what you consider to be reasonable goals for your own situation.

It is expected that these sets of performance criteria could replace standard job descriptions since they go so much further, spelling out precisely what a job entails and the tasks to be accomplished. Because of the complexity of most library jobs today, each grouping actually contains a mixture of measurable standards, qualitative standards, and task descriptions. To evaluate performance adequately, it is crucial that both employee and supervisor regularly document concrete examples that illustrate successful (or unsuccessful) performance as they arise, so that these can be cited in the annual performance review. This, however, does not have to be a formal process—dated notes slipped into a folder, with just enough detail to jog the memory, will do very well!

Note: When using the standards in this chapter (and indeed the standards for all positions included in this book), it will be necessary for the individual library to decide what percentage of the employee's time (and the corresponding weight to be given on the performance evaluation) should be allotted to each function. Each group of tasks included in any one job module could comprise anywhere from 5 percent to 70 percent or more of an individual employee's performance criteria, depending on the needs of the library and the other duties assigned to the specific individual. For example, if the employee only helps out in a department on weekends, the weight assigned to those tasks would obviously be light; but if the person is assigned to work in a specific area full-time, then more would be expected, and the weight would be greater. In addition, not all the tasks defined would necessarily be done by one individual; they are merely composites of typical tasks performed in those functional areas.

UNIT/DEPARTMENT/DIVISION HEAD

I. Supervision and administration of unit/department/division
    A. Planning and assessment
        1. General planning
            Includes, but is not limited to:

            Anticipates needs, problems; recognizes trends

            Keeps informed about issues, services, and innovations related to unit/department/division

            Evaluates/relates these ideas, procedures, or projects to the library/department/division's mission

            Establishes realistic goals and objectives

            Informs staff and administration of ideas, plans, policies, and procedures

            Establishes priorities; develops necessary plans, including staffing needs, for the implementation of these services, innovative ideas, or solutions to problems

            Assessment: staff evaluations; supervisor observations and record-keeping

        2. General assessment
            Includes but is not limited to:

            Assesses self, staff, departmental effectiveness, and services on a regular basis through appropriate means necessary for provision of the best service (e.g., consultations, surveys, questionnaires, peer evaluation, counseling, etc.)

            Assessment: patron responses, assessment results, evaluations, supervisor observations and record-keeping, staff evaluations

3. Planning/assessment documents
   a. Unit plan (Planning)
      Includes, but is not limited to:

      Plan is clearly written and follows library's prescribed format

      Plan is thorough: provides for ongoing functions, addresses plans for future and correction of problems

      Plan is specific, outcomes are observable/measurable

      Shows innovative approaches to meeting library/department/division objectives

      Staff is involved in development of plan

      All deadlines for submission of documents met

      Assessment: portfolio, record-keeping by supervisor and at next level

   b. Budget (Planning)
      Includes, but is not limited to:

      Budget includes new and present staff, materials, maintenance, equipment, and all supplies necessary for operation of department or unit

      Follows prescribed format

      Budget is thorough: allows for ongoing functions and implementation of plans for coming year, and addresses correction of problems

      Budget is tied to unit plan

      All deadlines are met

      Assessment: portfolio; feedback from administration/Budget Office, etc.; record-keeping by supervisor or other involved personnel

    c. Annual report (Assessment)
        Includes, but is not limited to:

        Follows prescribed format including accomplishments and failures tied to the year's unit plan

        Includes information on all operations of unit/department/division

        Report is clearly written and succinct

        All deadlines are met

        Assessment: portfolio, record-keeping by supervisor and at next level

  B. Manages operation of department

    1. Establishes departmental policy and procedures
        Includes, but is not limited to:

        Develops and revises policies; presents to supervisor or other appropriate administrators for approval and distribution

        Maintains updated departmental policies and procedures manual in a location accessible to all subordinates

        Keeps staff informed of changes

        Sees that updates to Library Policies and Procedures Manual are filed promptly and that manual is kept in a location accessible to all

        Assessment: peer and staff feedback, supervisor inspection of policies and procedures documents

    2. Organizes, staffs, and directs work of department
        Includes, but is not limited to:

Implements (carries out) plans

Communicates information, directions, changes, etc.

Prepares equitable and timely staffing schedules, including preparing weekly changes in advance, making daily changes as needed, and seeing that all hours are sufficiently covered

Regularly directs and helps to organize work of department:

- work area is organized
- workflow is well organized
- necessary manuals, materials, etc., are available, up-to-date, easily located
- tasks are distributed equitably

Identifies and works to solve problems

Gathers information and makes decisions on a timely basis

Is thoroughly familiar with the work being done by each staff member

Is readily available to staff for consultation and help

Is careful to see that all employees are working productively

Assessment: peer/staff/patron feedback, supervisor observations

3. Ensures maintenance of departmental infrastructure
Includes, but is not limited to:

Anticipates needs and takes steps to ensure that all staff have necessary supplies and equipment

Ensures that maintenance contracts for equipment in the unit/department/division are kept up-to-date

Handles maintenance/repair requests promptly

Follows prescribed procedures for requesting/ordering

Coordinates or provides input into scheduling of building maintenance tasks so that work is interrupted as little as possible
Assessment: staff/peer/vendor/Business Office/ Maintenance Department feedback; supervisor observations

4. Personnel management
   Includes, but is not limited to:

   Plans for staffing needs; writes job descriptions for new positions

   Follows procedures carefully in interviewing and hiring full- and part-time personnel

   Trains new staff members carefully and thoroughly

   Provides clear instructions regarding work assignments

   Motivates and encourages personnel

   Suggests opportunities for involvement in faculty/staff development activities and encourages participation

   Provides staff with regular informal feedback on job performance during the year

   Documents staff performance as appropriate

   Promptly deals with conflicts among staff and resolves them equitably

   Reviews job descriptions regularly; updates them after consultation with staff

   Develops, with staff, criteria for performance

evaluations

Formally evaluates staff annually in an objective, timely, and equitable manner, following established library procedures and schedules

Treats all staff members with respect, tact, and impartiality

Assessment: peer and staff feedback, staff evaluations based on above criteria; supervisor observations and record-keeping

C. Acts as communication channel between department staff and administration, and other library departments (communicates up, down, and laterally). Keeps staff informed of all matters they need to know to perform their jobs
Includes, but is not limited to:

Meets regularly (formally or informally) with members of department

Conducts efficient and effective meetings

Willingly considers new ideas and/or suggestions from subordinates, peers, or supervisors, and responds thoughtfully and respectfully

Brings issues concerning department before appropriate administrators

Communicates decisions/information from meetings to staff in a clear and timely manner

Oral and written communications are accurate, effective, and appropriate to the purpose they are designed to fulfill

Takes information, comments, questions from staff to library administrators

Is seldom absent or late for meetings at which attendance is expected, and then only when absolutely necessary

Assessment: staff evaluations based on above criteria; supervisor observations and record-keeping ; peer and staff feedback

REFERENCE LIBRARIAN[1]

> *Note: The task of Reference Librarians is to assist library users in locating information, either from resources available within the library, or from some other source. The behaviors identified below, representing* standard performance, *are not meant to be inclusive: they are merely examples of the conduct expected of those who are assigned to Reference duty.*

A. Responsibilities to library users

    1. Conveys a warm, yet professional attitude
        Includes, but is not limited to:

        Listens carefully, asks questions as necessary in order to be sure s/he understands what is needed

        Treats all users with equal courtesy and consideration, is tactful and nonjudgmental

        Avoids behaviors, casual remarks, or jokes that could be construed as sexist

        Invites approach by acknowledging the presence of library patrons as they enter the Reference area (makes eye contact, smiles, etc.)

        Appears to be truly concerned with the user's request

        Tries to instill confidence in users who project or express feelings of inadequacy, etc.

        Encourages user to return to the desk for further help if his/her information need is still not satisfied after s/he has followed the suggestions first provided

        Readily asks colleagues for help when needed

    2. Gives full attention to the primary task
        Includes, but is not limited to:

While on duty at the desk, avoids personal conversations (including phone calls)

Keeps consultations with other staff members as brief as possible

If engaged in other work while at the desk, does not become so absorbed as to ignore patrons

Notices and approaches individuals who look like they may need help

3. Embodies the qualities expected of a good teacher
    Includes, but is not limited to:

    Chooses sources appropriate to the question asked and to the questioner's objectives and level of expertise

    Accompanies user to information source whenever possible, and shows him/her how to search effectively

    Makes certain that the user understands how to operate equipment or use the recommended source before leaving him/her to work alone

    Provides correct information in response to brief queries

    Uses all available resources (as appropriate), including Internet, print, online, telephone, etc.

    Follows up with information seeker to be sure that needs have been adequately met

    Prepares guides to information resources and keeps them current

    Takes responsibility for self-training in areas identified as personal weaknesses

    Stays up-to-date on new resources as they are added to the collection or to which access has been provided

Suggests other support services (such as ILL, scheduled information literacy classes, regional cooperative borrowing arrangements, etc.) when appropriate

Provides clear directions to users trying to locate materials

Effectively uses and teaches functions of the library's online system and other computer databases

B. Responsibilities to the library and coworkers
1. Treats colleagues with consideration and respect
    Includes, but is not limited to:

    Punctually arrives at the desk for scheduled hours

    Gives sufficient advance notice when unable to be present for scheduled hours, or arranges for a substitute

    Remains available near desk during duty periods, except when s/he must leave in order to accommodate the needs of a specific patron request

    When briefly leaving the desk during duty hours, lets colleagues know (why, where, and for how long)

    Does not speak negatively about the library, the profession, or colleagues

    Records scheduled vacation, sick leave, etc., on departmental calendar

    Arrives for meetings on time, and constructively participates in discussion

    Keeps colleagues informed of own work status and/or developments that might affect their work

    Interacts effectively with colleagues; cooperates and collaborates to achieve departmental goals

    Accepts and acts on constructive criticism from supervisor and coworkers

Does not ignore problems or leave them for others to take care of (e.g., copier out of paper, microfilm reader/printer needing toner), but deals with them promptly whenever necessary

2. Satisfactorily performs tasks needed in order for the library to function efficiently and meet its institutional goals
    Includes, but is not limited to:

Collects and maintains statistical records necessary to evaluate accomplishment of service goals and objectives

Creates/maintains attractive and useful departmental WWW pages

Knows library policies and procedures; accurately interprets them, and clearly and courteously communicates policies to patrons and staff as necessary

On the infrequent occasions when exceptions to library policy are made, uses good judgment in making these decisions

Identifies and recommends for purchase materials appropriate to the reference/general collection

Identifies items which should be weeded and initiates orders for newer editions, etc.

Checks ILL request forms received at the Reference Desk for completeness and accuracy

Encourages patrons to utilize fully the resources available or accessible locally before choosing Interlibrary Loan

Uses time, supplies, and equipment effectively and efficiently

Completes projects within agreed-upon standards of accuracy and timeliness

Sees to it that any Reference Department assistants (such as student or part-time workers) are engaged in productive work while they are on duty

Shelves reference books whenever necessary

Assessment: peer and patron feedback, supervisor observations, portfolio items, self-evaluation

LIBRARY/BIBLIOGRAPHIC
INSTRUCTION COORDINATOR

Note: As mentioned earlier, for all positions included in this book, the individual library must decide what percentage of the employee's time should be allotted to each function. For example, the Library/Bibliographic Instruction Coordinator would certainly have as part of his or her performance standards the Unit Head and Library/ Bibliographic Instruction Provider modules, and, in many libraries, also the Reference Librarian module.

A.   Manages library instructional programs
     Includes, but is not limited to:

   Takes primary responsibility for providing library instruction

   Matches instructional requests from teaching faculty with available and qualified staff members, checks space availability, then confirms appointments within 2 working days

   Maintains up-to-date and easily accessible schedule of classes and tours

   Sees to it that instructional facilities and equipment are properly maintained and kept in good order, always ready for the next scheduled session

   Troubleshoots equipment in need of repairs; either repairs or schedules service calls within 24 hours

   Designs program evaluation forms, assures that evaluation is done on an ongoing basis, and analyzes results so that feedback can be used to improve curriculum

   Sees that needed equipment is ordered promptly, and follows up on delivery and/or damage

Prepares and disseminates clear, up-to-date policies and procedures governing the instructional program

Coordinates instructional planning with library staff; always keeps colleagues informed of program changes and equipment problems that may affect them

Serves as a responsive and cooperative liaison between library and teaching faculty with regard to library instruction services provided

Provides statistical and evaluative reports to library administration as scheduled or requested

B.   Oversees preparation of instructional materials
     Includes, but is not limited to:

Serves as consultant and/or writes and produces instructional materials, handouts, guides, videos, etc.

Monitors materials produced in-house for consistency, attractiveness, and informational quality

Sees to it that sufficient quantities of instructional materials are on hand and available at all times to staff members who need them

Keeps literature racks in Reference Department filled with appropriate user guides

Maintains current copies of all user guides on library WWW page

Reviews instructional materials on a systematic basis to determine when updating or revision is needed

Takes responsibility for keeping up-to-date with desktop publishing software and for training/assisting other staff in use of this technology

C.   Plans for future instructional needs
      Includes, but is not limited to :

      Formally solicits feedback from all segments of the faculty to determine changing library instructional needs (at a minimum, annually; more often preferred)

      Takes the lead in planning/designing new curriculum and programs

      Proactively participates in evaluation and selection/recommendation of new equipment to be used in library instruction program

      Participates in conferences, peer group meetings, etc., and shares information obtained with other staff, so that current trends may be used to improve the library's instructional program as appropriate

      Assessment: peer/faculty/student feedback, supervisor observations, portfolio items, self-evaluation

LIBRARY/BIBLIOGRAPHIC INSTRUCTION PROVIDER

Note: The items below, representing standard performance, *are not inclusive: they are merely examples of
the kinds of behavior expected of those who provide bibliographic instruction.*

A. Handles instructional responsibilities in an organized, efficient manner
Includes, but is not limited to:

Encourages faculty to schedule classes as far in advance
as possible

Assists in coordination of scheduling by promptly en-
tering dates/times on library instruction calendar

Prepares presentations (or updates those previously
used) well in advance of scheduled date

Is punctual in meeting class at prearranged location in
the library

Uses evaluation forms to get feedback from attendees
at every session conducted

Removes materials used during session from the Library
Instruction Room/Lab and straightens area after class has
departed

Tabulates and summarizes evaluations and provides information to Coordinator in library-specified format
within 2 days after session has occurred

B. Provides a high-quality instructional program
Includes, but is not limited to:

Consults with professor in advance regarding content,
in order to ensure relevancy and usefulness

Encourages instructor to be present during session if at all possible

Presents a program that is clear, accurate, focused, and carefully geared to student needs

Times presentation so that it is completed within the period allotted

Finds ways to make students active participants, rather than passive listeners

Makes the effort to be warm, personable, enthusiastic about the subject; uses appropriate humor if possible

Remains available for questions and/or followup at the conclusion of the presentation

Provides class with personal e-mail address, office phone number, or other appropriate means of contacting instruction provider later, in case there are additional questions

Solicits feedback from professor regarding success and usefulness of presentation, including suggestions for future modifications in content

C.   Uses instructional media appropriately and effectively
     Includes, but is not limited to:

Prepares (or arranges for preparation of) helpful and attractive overheads, WWW pages, and/or other instructional media as needed

Checks room in advance to be sure all needed equipment is present and in good working order

Provides useful, clearly written handouts for session attendees

Uses instructional media that are concise and well designed and show good use of graphics

Ensures that handouts in sufficient quantity for all attendees are ready well in advance of the scheduled presentation

Shares instructional materials with coworkers

Assessment: BI evaluation forms, instructor feedback, peer feedback, supervisor observations

SPECIAL COLLECTIONS LIBRARIAN/ARCHIVIST

A. Takes responsibility for proactively developing Special Collections
    Includes, but is not limited to:

    Obtains appropriate oral histories

    Solicits and negotiates the donation of appropriate papers and manuscripts

    Locates other materials of potential value and acquires them or recommends them for purchase

    Establishes systems and procedures to ensure that complete collections of archival materials (appropriate to the specific library) are being received, and monitors these systems on a regular basis

    Makes regular progress on and/or completes in a timely manner any special projects assigned or accepted

B. Manages collection effectively
    Includes, but is not limited to:

    Keeps collections policies up-to-date

    Maintains clear signage for ease of location by staff and patrons

    Processes new material promptly (e.g., within one month of receipt)

    Works cooperatively with Cataloging Department so that materials are cataloged promptly

    Sees to it that materials are shelved weekly

    Monitors stack maintenance in order to determine that materials are in good order, to see that necessary shifting is completed promptly, etc.

    Establishes appropriate procedures to safeguard materials entrusted to the care of the department

Maintains accurate statistics and reports them promptly according to established schedules

Knows and follows accepted techniques for stabilization/ preservation/repair of all materials

C. Ensures that Special Collections materials are used to the fullest extent
Includes, but is not limited to :

Provides appropriate levels of training and information to other public services staff

Provides reference service for collection on a regular, announced schedule

Maintains records of restrictions on access and applies them as necessary

Responds immediately to requests for assistance from other public services desks

Provides in-depth assistance by appointment to scholars, researchers, journalists, etc., who wish to use the collection

Keeps up-to-date on new technologies; studies and recommends implementation of those that promise to improve access cost-effectively and/or to contribute to preservation efforts

Prepares displays or uses other means to increase the visibility of, and interest in, Special Collections

Participates in local/national/regional historical associations; accepts opportunities to speak to appropriate groups

Creates/maintains effective and informative departmental WWW pages

Assessment: peer and patron feedback, supervisor observations, portfolio items, self-evaluation.

ACQUISITIONS/SERIALS/COLLECTION
DEVELOPMENT LIBRARIAN

A.   Manages functions of the department
     Includes, but is not limited to:

     Reviews budget reports daily/weekly/monthly

     Monitors expenditures/encumbrances to ensure that funds are being expended at an appropriate rate

     Prepares coherent and persuasive written justifications for requested supplemental funding or extraordinary expenditures

     Oversees and annually reviews allocation of funds according to subject area, academic department, etc.

     Keeps appropriate parties (academic department heads, subject bibliographers, etc.) informed of current budget allocation status on a monthly basis

     Supervises verification/ordering/receipt/bindery fund disbursement processes to ensure that correct procedures are being followed

     Reviews verification/ordering/receipt/bindery fund disbursement processes on a systematic basis to determine when updating/revision/streamlining is needed

     Works cooperatively with Business Office and Cataloging/Processing Department so that materials are received promptly and flow smoothly and rapidly through the system to the shelves

     Is an expert user of the library's online system, able to answer all staff questions and train new staff effectively

     Makes sound decisions on selection of vendors based on judgement of most important factors relevant to specific situation (e.g., delivery speed/reliability/availability vs. cost/discount, etc.)

Ensures that written acknowledgements of gifts are promptly dispatched

Sees that up-to-date printouts of periodicals holdings are provided to designated service units per established schedule

Orders needed supplies and equipment promptly and follows up on delivery problems and/or damage

Prepares and disseminates clear, up-to-date policies and procedures governing the acquisitions process

Provides statistical/financial/evaluative reports to library administration as scheduled or requested

B. Collection development and evaluation
    Includes, but is not limited to:

Scans reviewing media/retrospective catalogs on an on-going basis in order to identify potential additions to the collection

Assists in identifying materials to be moved to storage

Reviews materials received/identified via approval plans, publishers' advertising, user/faculty/departmental requests, gifts, and other sources in order to determine whether these materials should be added to the collection

Researches ownership vs. access options, evaluates cost/benefit, and decides which option is appropriate for various materials needed by the library's users

Utilizes information sources available (use studies, ILL requests, accreditation documents, staff feedback, etc.) in order to determine which subscriptions should be renewed/dropped

Knows and uses professionally accepted standard criteria to evaluate/supervise evaluations of the adequacy of library collections on an annual basis

Analyzes results of evaluations and uses data to improve the collection and to make future collection development decisions

Regularly initiates and supervises weeding projects

Makes unneeded materials available through established gifts and exchanges networks, library sales, etc.

Sees to it that sufficient quantities of materials-ordering forms, etc., are on hand and available to those who need them at all times

Maintains departmental WWW page, including up-to-date materials-ordering template, etc.

C.   Plans for future needs of the department and library
Includes, but is not limited to :

Keeps up-to-date on new acquisitions technologies; studies and recommends implementation of those that promise cost-effective improvement of departmental effectiveness

Solicits feedback from all segments of the faculty/community/staff to determine changing curriculum/informational needs

Proactively participates in evaluation and selection of new equipment to be used in the department

Participates in conferences, peer group meetings, etc., and shares information obtained with other staff, so that current trends may be used to improve the library's acquisitions procedures

Identifies areas in library's online acquisitions module that could be improved; recommends changes to be included in future system upgrades

Assessment: peer/user/Business Office/vendor feedback, supervisor observations, portfolio items, self-evaluation.

CATALOGER

A. Cataloging
Includes, but is not limited to:

Is an expert user of all modules of the library's automated system that are needed in this position; able to answer all staff questions and train new workers effectively

Is a sophisticated user of the OCLC cataloging system

Performs full original cataloging of books and materials [in x formats] with an error rate of less than 5%, using MARC format, LC subject headings, etc.

Prepares cataloging data for input; assigns codes and tags accurately

Performs difficult copy cataloging with an error rate of less than 1%

Catalogs an average of x items per month

Establishes correct authority records for names, series, subject, uniform titles, etc.

Locates correct, relevant records in OCLC or other databases to assist with cataloging

Effectively supervises copy cataloging done by subordinates and able to answer their questions

Reviews cataloging done by subordinates on a systematic basis to check accuracy; corrects them as necessary

Supervises physical processing of materials and checks to be sure work is being done accurately and neatly (label printing, ownership marking, security stripping, etc.)

Works cooperatively with departmental colleagues, Acquisitions, and public service areas so that materials flow smoothly and rapidly through the system to the shelves

Prepares and provides statistical and other reports to library administration as scheduled or requested

Takes responsibility for keeping up-to-date on revisions in cataloging rules/practices

Shares information about new cataloging rules/practices with supervisor and colleagues, and applies this knowledge to the work as appropriate

Supervises/performs quality control checking of materials ready to go to stacks

B.   Database maintenance
     Includes, but is not limited to:

Corrects and resolves problems related to obsolete, conflicting, or incorrect older cataloging

Identifies items that need recataloging/reclassification and handles the work promptly and correctly

Notices and corrects holdings and other errors in bibliographic databases

Adds copies/volumes promptly and correctly

Promptly and correctly processes withdrawals

Follows correct procedures for editing and deleting records in OCLC and library's online system

Checks LC subject headings changes as they occur and updates local database on a regular basis

Assessment: peer user feedback, supervisor observations and sample checking of work, portfolio items, self-evaluation

GOVERNMENT DOCUMENTS LIBRARIAN

A. Proactively develops the documents collection
    Includes, but is not limited to:

    Selects new series and other government documents for the library collection in accordance with departmental and library collection policies

    Keeps up-to-date on curricular and program changes in order to select appropriate materials for the documents collection

    Takes responsibility for keeping up-to-date on Internet-accessible sources of government information and considers this when deciding whether to maintain paper copies

    Evaluates materials for possible weeding and/or transfer to storage

B. Manages the documents collection effectively
    Includes, but is not limited to:

    Maintains clear and accurate signage for ease of location by staff and patrons

    Checks annual printout of item selections for accuracy and makes item additions or deletions

    Removes superseded materials as replacements are received

    Works cooperatively with Cataloging Department so that materials to be cataloged are handled promptly

    Sees to it that materials are shelved at least weekly

    Reviews filing systems, processing and ordering procedures, etc., at least annually, in order to find ways to streamline and increase efficiency

Monitors stack maintenance in order to determine that materials are in good order, to see that necessary shifting is completed promptly, etc.

Compiles accurate statistics and reports them promptly according to established schedules

Initiates and supervises weeding projects, transfers to storage, etc.

Proactively participates in evaluation and selection of new equipment to be used in the department

C.   Ensures that the documents collection is used to the fullest extent
Includes, but is not limited to:

Evaluates new materials as they are received in order to determine appropriate level of bibliographic access needed and best location within the library

Provides appropriate levels of training and information to other public services staff

Identifies and orders necessary bibliographic tools and indexes in order to ensure convenient and useful access to the documents collection

Gives specialized instruction and reference service for collection

Responds immediately to requests from other public services desks for assistance

Works cooperatively with other library departments to ensure that best possible access to the collection is provided

Keeps up-to-date on new technologies; studies and recommends implementation of those that promise to improve access cost-effectively, relieve stack congestion, etc.

Oversees annual ordering and distribution of tax forms

Prepares and disseminates clear, up-to-date policies and procedures governing the documents collection

Finds appropriate ways to keep peers, campus, and wider community aware of the availability of government documents (both in the collection and via the Internet) and promotes their use (e.g. displays, newsletters, handouts, speaking engagements, departmental WWW page)

Assists ILL department with verification of requested documents not owned by the library

Is able to refer users when library does not have what is needed (to the most convenient regional depository, local branches of federal/state agencies, federal bookstores, etc.)

Makes good use of promotional materials (such as posters, stickers, catalogs) supplied to depository libraries

Protects and facilitates access to the documents collection by the general public

Assessment: peer and patron feedback, supervisor observations, portfolio items, self-evaluation.

D. Serves as an effective liaison between the library and the GPO, state documents providers, etc.
   Includes, but is not limited to:

   Maintains collection in accordance with the latest editions of the *Federal Depository Manual* and *Instructions to Depository Libraries*, state requirements, etc.

   Keeps current on Depository Library Program policies, trends in document librarianship, etc., and makes changes as needed

Sees that GPO and other deposit accounts are always maintained at an adequate level

Is completely prepared for the quinquennial depository library inspection and receives ratings of Good or Excellent in all categories

Supplies regional depository with lists of items available for exchange or being discarded

Responds promptly to all requests from the Depository Library Program (e.g., the GPO Biennial Survey, item surveys, etc.)

Assessment: GPO feedback, supervisor observations

CIRCULATION LIBRARIAN

Note: Among academic libraries at least, the current practice increasingly seems to be that of employing paraprofessionals to head up Circulation Departments. If there is a professional Circulation Librarian on staff, the individual is usually very much a working supervisor. Therefore, standards for a Circulation Librarian could be developed by selecting and adapting examples from among those included under Unit/Department/Division Head *and in Chapter 3 under* Circulation Assistant.

INTERLIBRARY LOAN LIBRARIAN

Note: If the library is not large, and there is only one ILL Librarian, the standards for this position would also include all or most of the items included under Unit/Department/Division Head. No attempt was made to duplicate them here.

A. Possesses an expert knowledge of all aspects of the OCLC/RLIN/ARIEL/regional ILL system(s), etc., as well as those aspects of the local library's automated system that pertain to this position

Includes, but is not limited to:

Independently and thoroughly trains new workers to use systems

Makes constructive suggestions for needed system revisions when upgrades/changes are being considered

Is able to resolve all system use problems for subordinates

Is responsible for quickly gaining familiarity with all upgrades and changes, and for communicating these to subordinates

B. Coordinates/performs lending operations
    Includes, but is not limited to:

    Ensures that lending requests on systems used are re-
    sponded to daily

    Supervises process of retrieving requested materials from
    local collection and, prior to mailing, checks to be sure
    correct material is being sent

    Sees that request record is updated in system when ma-
    terial is shipped

    Ensures that overdue notices are prepared weekly when
    needed

    Reviews overdue notices for accuracy prior to mailing

    Daily oversees processing of system message files

C. Coordinates/performs borrowing operations
    Includes, but is not limited to:

    Supervises verification of ILL requests

    Successfully handles difficult verifications, and/or re-
    quests additional information from requestor

    Ensures that all full-text computer databases available
    are checked before request is made to other libraries

    Supervises entry of borrowing requests into system

    Accesses/knows policies of lending libraries and uses
    this knowledge in order to select the most appropriate
    lenders

    Knows of and utilizes other resources (such as commer-
    cial document suppliers) whenever necessary or appro-
    priate

    Checks and processes invoices for lending/document
    purchase charges within 2 working days

Ensures that accurate and up-to-date records of materials borrowed from other libraries are maintained, and that delinquent borrowers are notified as soon as possible

D. Other department duties
Includes, but is not limited to:

Takes responsibility for keeping up-to-date on ILL and copyright law trends and changes; communicates new information to colleagues and applies knowledge to job as appropriate

Maintains copyright records and enforces copyright regulations

Keeps complete and accurate statistical records on ILL operations

Supplies accurate reports to administration/other departments as scheduled or requested

Sees to it that sufficient quantities of ILL forms are on hand and available at all times to those who need them

Maintains departmental WWW page, including up-to-date ILL request template, etc.

Knows and clearly communicates ILL policies and procedures to users and staff

Identifies and recommends for purchase materials that the library does not own, but which are frequently requested by local users

Encourages patrons to fully utilize the resources available or accessible locally, before choosing interlibrary loan

When sufficient time for ILL is not available, offers to refer users to nearest libraries that own the needed materials

Makes sure that subordinates are engaged in productive work while they are on duty

Assessment: peer and patron feedback, supervisor observations, portfolio items, self-evaluation

SYSTEMS LIBRARIAN

A. Manages all library automation systems
    Includes, but is not limited to:

Takes responsibility for self-training in all aspects of library systems (e.g., through attendance at workshops sponsored by service providers, etc.)

Proactively participates in systems design, equipment evaluation, and selection process

Ensures that specified equipment is ordered promptly and follows up on delivery or damage problems

Sees that site preparation, installation, implementation, and testing of new systems is done in a timely and efficient manner

Successfully integrates new computer systems with existing systems

Takes steps to ensure that networks are secure and that unauthorized access is blocked

Maintains and updates system promptly whenever needed (e.g., loan periods, closed dates, passwords, IP addresses, documentation, etc.)

Quickly and successfully troubleshoots computer equipment and systems malfunctions; repairs (or arranges for repairs) promptly

Checks weekly for reports that need to be deleted, system errors, problem reports, diskspace, etc.

Develops and implements plans and procedures for recovery from system failures

Performs database/systems backups on schedule

Systematically and thoroughly trains staff in equipment cleaning and maintenance procedures

B. Coordinates with user and vendor constituencies
    Includes, but is not limited to:

    Coordinates systems upgrades with all staff affected

    Acts promptly on recommendations of administrators, and library's Automation Committee, staff requests for assistance, etc.

    Works cooperatively with campus Computer Center

    Coordinates automation planning with library staff; consistently strives to keep colleagues informed of systems changes that may affect their work

    Serves as a responsive and cooperative liaison between library and service providers, local/regional consortia, etc.

    Consults with other staff before making decisions that will directly affect them

    Advises and assists other library staff with WWW page construction

C. Provides automation-related staff support
    Includes, but is not limited to:

    Provides appropriate levels of training and documentation for staff

    Installs updated and demo versions of electronic information products and software within 1 week of receipt

    Serves as consultant and/or writes and produces user education materials related to automation products

    Informs staff well in advance of systems upgrades and changes; provides needed documentation prior to implementation

    Shares information on new technologies, feedback on usage of CD-ROM products, etc., with library staff

Completes projects within agreed-upon time frame

Sets up labs for training and BI, arranges short-term computer connectivity for out-of-building demos, etc.

Assessment: peer/patron/vendor feedback, supervisor observations, portfolio items, self-evaluation

EXTENSION/OFF-CAMPUS SERVICES LIBRARIAN

A.   Ensures that distance education instructors and users are made aware of available library support services and are provided access to these services
Includes, but is not limited to:

Supplies information about library support services to every off-campus instructor at least one week prior to the beginning of the next quarter/semester

Creates attractive and informative materials describing available library support options for distance education students

Distributes flyers, brochures and other advertising materials to all off-campus students every quarter/semester

Devises means to ensure that services can be accessed in a wide variety of ways (e.g., 800 number, paper and electronic request forms, announcement of fax numbers and e-mail addresses, etc.)

Maintains departmental WWW page, electronic versions of off-campus request form, etc., so that these information sources are always up-to-date

Seeks and finds opportunities to disseminate information about library support for distance education through other means (e.g., personal networking with faculty and librarians in communities served, articles in local media, listserv communications, special memos to faculty)

Proactively encourages instructors and students to gain access to the Internet

Creates and distributes informational materials designed to help off-campus students and faculty make optimum use of Internet resources

Develops clear policies, procedures, and plans for provision of off-campus library support, and revises these as needed

Informs instructors and students of regional cooperative borrowing arrangements and provides means to access these services

B. Provides library materials and services appropriate to the off-campus classes offered
Includes, but is not limited to:

Takes responsibility for keeping up-to-date on curriculum changes, planned course offerings, etc.

Systematically seeks input from faculty and students regarding materials/services needed

Keeps up-to-date on library resources available locally as well as at libraries in the vicinity of off-campus sites

When necessary, is able to refer off-campus students to appropriate libraries in their own area

Consults/maintains contact with librarians at cooperating libraries in order to learn more about the kinds of materials needed by off-campus students

Purchases/recommends for purchase materials and equipment for off-site or cooperating libraries that will increase access to information and/or are relevant to curriculum needs

Materials assembled in response to student requests are ready for shipping within one week of receipt of request

Balances considerations of expense, timeliness, and student needs in order to select the most cost-effective mode of delivery

If library does not own needed materials, submits ILL requests within 2 business days of receipt of request

Ensures that off-site reserve materials (already owned by the library) are available for student use no later than the beginning of the second week of classes

Promptly schedules library instruction sessions in response to request from course instructor

Constantly seeks ways to streamline and improve services to make them more efficient, timely, and responsive to student and faculty needs

C.   Other departmental responsibilities
     Includes, but is not limited to:

Is alert to opportunities to secure extra-institutional support, and takes advantage of them (e.g., writes grant proposals, negotiates with other departments/local agencies to provide services, etc.)

Maintains regular contact with distance education sites

Coordinates courier services to sites

Oversees billing of students for chargeable services and materials

Ensures that payments received are credited within one day of receipt

Maintains accurate statistical records on program

Provides statistical reports to administrators as scheduled or requested

Retrieves or arranges for retrieval of reserve materials from off-campus sites within 2 weeks of the end of quarter/semester

Assessment: instructor/student/peer feedback, supervisor observations, self-evaluation

BRANCH LIBRARIAN (PUBLIC LIBRARY)[2]

A. Proactively develops the branch materials collection
    Includes, but is not limited to:

    Takes responsibility for developing a broad knowledge
    of the world and the ways in which it is portrayed
    through books and other materials, by engaging in regu-
    lar personal reading in many subject areas, scanning re-
    views, talking to patrons, etc.

    Is familiar with the collection already available in the
    branch and uses that knowledge to select items that will
    expand the breadth of the collection, and not duplicate
    materials already held

    Regularly surveys the collection to identify areas in
    which more materials are needed

    Continuously studies the demographics and needs of the
    population served by the branch, and considers those
    factors when making materials selections

    Scans reviewing media/retrospective catalogs on an on-
    going basis in order to identify potential additions to
    the collection

    Follows library policies and procedures for ordering new
    materials

    Monitors expenditures/encumbrances to ensure that
    funds are being expended at an appropriate rate

    Knows and uses professionally accepted standard crite-
    ria to select materials and evaluate the collection

    Regularly initiates and supervises weeding projects

    Makes unneeded materials available according to estab-
    lished library system policies (e.g., gifts and exchange,
    donations to local agencies, library sales)

B. Takes steps to ensure that users' needs are met
    Includes, but is not limited to:

    Conveys a warm, yet professional attitude toward library patrons

    Treats all users with equal courtesy and consideration

    Listens carefully, asks questions as necessary in order to be sure s/he understands what is needed

    Acknowledges the presence of library patrons as they enter the library

    Gives full attention to the task of public service

    - does not engage in lengthy personal conversations while on duty
    - keeps phone calls short
    - if engaged in other work while at the desk, does not become so absorbed as to ignore patrons
    - notices and approaches individuals who look like they may need help
    - remains available near desk during duty periods, except when s/he must leave in order to accommodate a specific patron request

    Is familiar with the collection already available in the branch and keeps up-to-date with new acquisitions

    Chooses sources appropriate to the question asked and to the questioner's objectives

    Uses all available resources (e.g. Internet, print, online, telephone, materials requested from Main Library) as appropriate

    Effectively uses and teaches functions of the library's online catalog system and other computer databases available

C. Serves as an effective liaison between the library and the community
    Includes, but is not limited to:

    Strives to find ways to position the branch as the primary information resource for the local community

    Conforms to library system standards of dress and behavior when at work or when otherwise representing the library to the public

    Seeks opportunities to speak and write about the library and its resources in the public forum

    Takes steps to improve oral and written communication skills if needed

    Regularly participates in local organizations and attends community activities

    Finds opportunities to meet and interact with local community leaders

    Plans programs for the branch that are of interest to the community and that respond to local needs

D. Performs tasks needed in order for the library to function efficiently and meet its institutional goals
    Includes, but is not limited to:

    Collects and maintains statistical records necessary to evaluate accomplishment of service goals and objectives

    Knows library system policies and procedures; accurately interprets them, and clearly and courteously communicates policies to patrons and staff as necessary

    Uses time, supplies, and equipment effectively and efficiently

    Completes special projects within agreed-upon standards of accuracy and timeliness

Sees to it that subordinates are engaged in productive work while they are on duty

Ensures that building is always kept secure, clean, and attractive to patrons

Knows and upholds nationally recognized standards and professional codes of ethics regarding intellectual freedom, confidentiality of patron records, etc—and sees that all staff know and follow them

Assessment: peer and patron feedback, supervisor observations, portfolio items, self-evaluation

CHILDREN'S/YOUNG ADULT LIBRARIAN
(PUBLIC LIBRARY)

A. Proactively develops the children's/young adult materials collection
    Includes, but is not limited to:

    Takes responsibility for developing a broad knowledge of the world and the ways in which it is portrayed in juvenile/YA books and other media, by engaging in regular personal reading; scanning of reviews; exposure to movies, TV shows, and magazines geared to the age group; talking to children/teens, parents, teachers, school media specialists; etc.

    Is familiar with the children's/YA materials already available in the branch and uses that knowledge to select items that will expand the breadth of the collection or provide needed duplicates of popular items

    Regularly surveys the children's/YA collection to identify areas in which more materials are needed

    Continuously studies the demographics and needs of the youthful population served by the branch, and considers those factors when making materials selections

    Scans reviewing media and publishers' catalogs on an ongoing basis in order to identify potential additions to the collection

    Follows library policies and procedures for ordering new materials

    Monitors expenditures/encumbrances to ensure that funds are being expended at an appropriate rate

    Knows and uses professionally accepted standard criteria to select materials and evaluate the collection

    Regularly initiates and supervises weeding projects

Makes unneeded materials available according to established library system policies (e.g., donations to local agencies, library sales)

Keeps patrons informed of new acquisitions in various ways (displays, booktalks, flyers, bookmarks, etc.)

Reviews materials received as gifts in order to determine whether these should be added to the collection

Responds to complaints about materials in a prompt and respectful manner, and in accordance with library policies and national professional standards

B. Takes steps to ensure that the library needs of children and young adults are met
Includes, but is not limited to:

Conveys a warm, yet respectful and unpatronizing attitude toward young library users

Treats all users with equal courtesy and consideration

Listens carefully, asks questions as necessary in order to be sure s/he understands what is needed

Acknowledges the presence of children and teens as they enter the library

Plans regular programs, particularly when school is not in session, that simultaneously meet the informational/educational needs of young people and are fun and entertaining

Checks well in advance of scheduled programs to be sure that all supplies/materials/equipment needed are available

Gives full attention to public service when on duty

Is familiar with the current collection and keeps up-to-date with new acquisitions, so as to be able to readily recommend books to juvenile/YA patrons

Chooses sources appropriate to the question asked and to the questioner's age level and needs

Effectively uses and teaches functions of the library's online catalog system so that young users can be as independent as possible

C. Effectively manages the Children's/YA Area
Includes, but is not limited to:

Systematically and regularly evaluates library facilities available for children/YAs and for programs and services, and implements changes as indicated

Obtains feedback on programs/services/facilities from users and their parents, and uses the information thus acquired to make improvements/implement change as needed

Establishes clear goals, objectives, policies, and procedures, and communicates them to children/teens/parents/community

Continually seeks and finds ways to promote increased use of the Children's/YA Area

Uses time (including that of self, staff, and volunteers), supplies, and equipment effectively and efficiently

Ensures that the Children's/YA Area is always secure, clean, and attractive to patrons

Designs and creates displays that are attractive to children/YAs

Whenever possible, coordinates children's/YA programs with other branch programs in order to

- avoid noncompatible building uses (e.g., noisy programs scheduled at the same time as quiet ones)
- make it possible for parents to attend an adult program while their children are attending a program in another area

- ensure that sufficient staff are available to meet the needs of other library patrons while programs are in progress

D. Serves as an effective liaison between the library, the schools, and the community
Includes, but is not limited to:

Visits all schools in the library's service area at least twice each year

During school visits, presents well-planned and interesting programs to classes, to inform them about services and programs available for them at the public library, and to attract them to come

Completes school visit activities within the previously agreed-upon time frame, so as to cause minimal disruption to the classroom teacher's schedule

Conforms to library system standards of dress and behavior when at work or when otherwise representing the library

Takes steps to improve oral and written communication skills if needed

Seeks opportunities to speak and write about the library and its resources in the public forum (e.g., PTA meetings, school newspapers, local meetings of school media specialists)

Assessment: peer and patron feedback, supervisor observations, portfolio items, self-evaluation

LIBRARY MEDIA SPECIALIST[3]

A. Effectively manages the school media program/center
    Includes, but is not limited to:

    Systematically evaluates all aspects of facilities/programs/
    services/procedures, analyzes results, and implements
    changes as indicated

    Obtains feedback on program/services/facilities from all
    affected constituencies and uses the information thus ac-
    quired to make improvements/implement change as nec-
    essary

    Establishes clear goals, objectives, policies, and proce-
    dures, and communicates them to students/parents/
    teachers/administrators/community

    Arrives for all scheduled meetings on time and proact-
    ively participates in problem solving and discussions of
    issues

    Continually seeks and finds ways to promote increased
    use of the media center

    Creates and maintains an environment that encourages
    research, study, and learning

    Promptly troubleshoots and/or arranges for repair of
    malfunctioning equipment

    Follows local procedures for specifying/purchasing/or-
    dering/receiving materials and equipment

    Effectively trains and supervises staff/volunteers, and
    evaluates them objectively

    Maintains accurate statistics and financial records, and
    supplies reports to administrators as scheduled or re-
    quested

    Prepares annual budgets based on previously developed
    goals and objectives

Monitors expenditures/encumbrances to ensure that funds are being expended at an appropriate rate

Uses time (including that of self, staff, and volunteers), supplies, and equipment effectively and efficiently

B. Collection development/management/evaluation
    Includes, but is not limited to:

Scans appropriate reviewing media and other selection tools on an ongoing basis in order to identify potential additions to the collection

Adds to the media center collection in accordance with national standards and local needs/policies

Supervises processing of new materials and sees that processing is handled expeditiously, so that new materials are available for users as soon as possible

Keeps users informed of new acquisitions

Initiates and supervises weeding/inventory projects on an annual basis

Reviews materials received as gifts in order to determine whether these should be added to the collection

Acknowledges gifts promptly

Researches ownership vs. access options, evaluates cost/benefit and decides which alternative is appropriate for various materials needed by media center users

Knows and uses professionally accepted standard criteria to evaluate the adequacy of collections on at least an annual basis

Takes responsibility for ensuring that accurate circulation records are kept and that media center materials are returned when due, so that they are available for other users

Actively encourages classroom teachers to make greater use of media center materials within the instructional program

Responds to complaints about materials in a prompt and respectful manner, and in accordance with local policies and national professional standards

C. Possesses the qualities expected of a good teacher
Includes, but is not limited to:

Is a full participant in the instructional mission of the school

Consults with classroom teachers regarding content of planned media center instructional programs in order to ensure relevancy and usefulness

Prepares and submits neat, coherent, and detailed lesson plans that include clear goals and objectives for learning

Structures library media instruction so that it supports school/district curricular needs

Serves as a consultant to classroom teachers in developing instructional programs that utilize media

Functions as a local resource for current information on new information technologies, intellectual property issues, etc.

Knows and uses sound pedagogical principles in order to communicate instructional content to students effectively

Keeps up-to-date on current educational theory and incorporates knowledge of issues (such as learning/cognitive styles, etc.) into personal repertoire of teaching techniques

Prepares and presents material that is clear, accurate, and appropriate to the needs, interests, and abilities of students

Finds ways to make students active participants in learning, rather than passive receptors of information

Prepares helpful and attractive instructional aids (e.g., handouts, overheads, multimedia tutorials)

Checks equipment and materials in advance to be sure that everything needed is available and in good operating order

Maintains good discipline in the media center by utilizing classroom management techniques that encourage self-control

Conveys a warm, courteous, respectful, and professional attitude toward all users

Is punctual in meeting classes at prearranged locations and completes planned programs within expected time frame

When unable to fulfill a teaching commitment, gives all those affected sufficient advance notice and arranges for a competent substitute

Seeks and finds opportunities, both formal and informal, to share with colleagues information obtained from conferences, professional reading, etc.

Uses effective evaluation techniques to get feedback from students and teachers, and uses this information to improve future instruction

D. Plans for the future
    Includes, but is not limited to:

    Keeps up-to-date on new technologies; studies and recommends for purchase those technologies that promise cost-effective improvement of information retrieval and use, instruction, work productivity, etc.

Solicits feedback from teachers/local and district administrators/regional educational authorities to determine changing curriculum/information needs

Participates in local/regional/national conferences and other peer group meetings; shares information obtained with media center staff/teachers/administration, so that current trends can be evaluated and, if applicable, used to guide and improve the local program

Is aware of grant-writing opportunities and takes advantage of them in order to supplement funds/services available through normal funding channels

Participates in or leads local networking/resource-sharing initiatives

Assessment: portfolio items, teacher/student/staff/parent/ community feedback, principal observations

LIBRARY WEBMASTER[4]

A. Coordinates development and maintenance of library WWW pages
    Includes, but is not limited to:

    Creates/designs/implements attractive and functional WWW pages that meet library needs as specified and defined by administrators

    Suggests/implements new Web applications of potential benefit to the library

    Demonstrates expert knowledge of HTML, Java, and other Web software

    Convenes and chairs regular meetings of other library staff involved in Web page development for needs assessment, problem-solving, etc.

    Develops specifications and policies for style, standards, and design, and ensures that these documents are available to staff

    Monitors pages produced by staff for compliance/quality, and ensures that corrections are made as necessary

    Regularly checks and verifies accuracy of links on library Web pages and updates them as needed

    Designs and supports special WWW features as needed by the library

    Keeps current on new Web enhancements and evaluates their potential usefulness to the library

    Maintains specified statistics on Web use and supplies reports in accordance with specified deadlines

B. Supervises staff/community training
    Includes, but is not limited to:

Keeps current on Web software developments and provides appropriate information to staff

Conducts regular training sessions in various aspects of WWW page design and creation as needed

Consults with staff engaged in Web page development individually as needed

Evaluates new WWW search engines, keeps staff informed of new developments, and provides training in their effective use

Prepares and conducts Web demonstrations for other segments of the community as requested by administrators

Assessment: feedback from users, public services staff, Systems Librarian; supervisor observations

ACADEMIC ACHIEVEMENT, PROFESSIONAL GROWTH AND DEVELOPMENT, SERVICE TO THE INSTITUTION (ACADEMIC LIBRARY)

Note: Since policies for librarians with faculty rank vary widely, this section is presented only as an example of how these areas could be handled. When evaluating Service to the Institution and Professional Growth and Development, account should be taken of the fact that librarians are normally subject to a 40-hour work week/ 12-month schedule, and therefore do not have as much time to devote to these endeavors as do the teaching faculty.

Academic Achievement

A second master's degree in a field other than librarianship, information science, or media is required for appointment or promotion to Assistant Professor, Associate Professor, or full Professor status.

Since the teaching faculty automatically receive full credit in the area of **Academic Achievement** because they possess the terminal degree (i.e., PhD) in their field, librarians of these ranks who have the MLS degree and a second (subject) master's degree will also automatically achieve a full rating in the performance area of **Academic Achievement.** Those librarians who take additional formal coursework may get credit for them under the category of **Professional Growth.**

First-year librarians ranked as Instructors and those other Instructors *who are making normal progress*[5] toward their second master's degree may also receive a full rating in this category.

Professional Growth and Development

All professional librarians are expected to participate actively in their profession. This may take the form of professional development activities that involve the practical application of existing knowledge or the creation of new knowledge. All are expected to have a professional development agenda, to make progress annually in addressing it, and to maintain proper professional ethics.

For performance appraisal, the criteria for **Professional Growth and Development** will be considered relative to the individual's rank in the organization, with standards based on the requirements for promotion to the next level. Thus, more will be expected at the higher levels to merit a rating comparable to that for those who hold a lower rank.

The criteria below are arranged in categories according to the significance of the accomplishment, with Category A being the most significant.

Category A (most significant)
   Evidentiary sources, national:
   Publications
      Book; publication in national journals
   Presentations before national professional societies
   National editorial work
   E-list manager
   Committee member/officer in national/international organization
   Honors, awards (professional)
   Grants (substantial, competitive)
   Conducting national workshops

Category B (significant)
   Evidentiary sources, regional:

Publication in regional/state journals
Presentations before regional professional societies
Editorships (regional, state)
Honors, awards (professional)
Grants
Conducting regional workshops
Attending national conferences and workshops
Committee member/officer in regional/state/local organization
Course work for credit

Category C (least significant)
Evidentiary sources, local:
Publications
Local publications; newsletters; guides, handouts; video productions
Presentations (before local or in-house groups)
Editorships of local publications
Attending state/local workshops/conferences (required workshops not admissible)
Honors, awards (professional)
Grants (local)
Conducting local workshops
Course work, audited

Service to the Institution

Library faculty are expected to participate in service to the institution, which includes College/University Service and Community Service. The former generally will be considered more significant. The latter, whenever possible, should be related to the profession but can include citizenship (civic clubs, church organizations, etc.). IMPORTANT: See *Faculty Handbook* for requirements for promotion and tenure. In your self-evaluation, you must communicate the extent of your involvement in service, demonstrated activity, and the scope of your contributions.

The criteria below are arranged in categories according to the significance of participation, with Category A being the most significant:

I. College/University Service

Category A
Evidentiary sources:
Long-term committee chair (2 years or more)
Officer in campus organization
Ongoing assignment in student advisement
Faculty advisor to student group
Shows clear evidence of collegiality; volunteers to help other departments when needed
Honors, awards, special recognition for service to the institution
Active participant in college/university development activities, fund-raising, etc.
Designated, official representative of college/university at special events (e.g., speaker, presenter of awards, moderator of conference sessions, etc.)
Course instructor for a department other than the library (more than one session, not library instruction)

Category B
Evidentiary sources:
Senator (faculty senate)
Short-term committee chair (less than 2 years)
Active member of a committee with demonstrated output
Active member of campus organization with demon-

strated output

Course instructor or guest lecturer for a department other than the library (one session, not library instruction)

II. Community Service

Category A

Evidentiary sources:

Community service related to the profession

- work at Friends of Public Library book sale
- organizing/staffing library of church or civic organization
- presentations to local organizations about library, information technology, etc.
- helping to set up local community information system, etc.

Honors, awards for service to the community

Category B

Evidentiary sources:

Leadership role in community organization (officer, committee chair)

Active membership in community organization

NOTES

1. Prior to writing these standards for Reference Librarian, I consulted a draft version of the *Guidelines for Behavioral Performance of Reference and Information Services Professionals*. This document was developed by the RASD Ad Hoc Committee on Behavioral Guidelines for Reference and Information Services, and is due to be published soon. See Chapter 5 (under American Library Association) for more details.

2. For these standards for Branch Librarian, I made partial use of the profile of the "excellent librarian" developed by the librarians of Phoe-

nix (Ariz.) Public Library and reported in Ellen Altman and Sara Brown, "What Makes a Librarian Excellent? The View from Phoenix," *Public Libraries* 30 (July/August 1991): 208–217. An annotation of this article is included in Chapter 5.

3. In writing these standards for Library Media Specialist, I was guided by a document sent to me by Sharon Early, Library Media Coordinator, School District No. 7, Lee's Summit, Mo. The document, *Performance Based Library Media Specialist Evaluation* (January 1994), is used in that school district.

4. These job standards/tasks are based on a job vacancy notice at the University of Pennsylvania which was posted on the PACS-L internet listserv.

5. First-year Instructors may be exempted from beginning their second master's degree for the first year of employment only, on the assumption that they should have an opportunity to become accustomed to their new duties before again undertaking the rigors of graduate study. By the second year of employment, however, Instructors are expected to have been accepted for graduate study in an accredited institution; from then until the degree is received they should complete a minimum of 2 courses per year.

5.   Leads from the Literature

This is a somewhat eclectic collection of citations* since my goal is twofold: to provide leads to useful materials *and* to save readers from wasting their time obtaining some items that show up in a literature search, but which, when examined in this context, are really not very helpful. In other words, I looked for materials that would be useful to a library trying to write objective performance standards, and in the process of doing that I wanted to alert readers to the true substance of some citations that may sound promising, but which are not.

Because of this narrow focus, the annotations deliberately do not always address every aspect of each item. Therefore, if the note seems to express a generally negative conclusion about a specific article or book, it doesn't necessarily mean that the item has no value, but merely that, in my opinion, it is not useful for the purposes outlined in this book.

---

*Citations are generally from the mid-1980s to the present, but a few earlier items have been included if they seemed particularly valuable. The attempt here is to concentrate on evaluation of *personnel* rather than services; however some "service evaluation" materials have been included, either because they contained some elements relevant to the writing of performance standards, or because the titles are misleading and I hoped that, by annotating them, I could help readers screen them from their own literature retrieval if they wished to.

Furthermore, although I looked at many sources drawn from the general field of personnel evaluation, I chose to concentrate on citations from library literature because (a) few of the items I found seemed to deal with situations analogous enough to the library setting to be truly practical and useful, (b) if I'd chosen otherwise, the bibliography would have taken up more than half the book, and (c) this is, after all, a book for libraries! The items from outside the library field that I felt were sufficiently transferable or useful have been included.

Adams, M., and B. Judd. "Evaluating Reference Librarians: Using Goal Analysis as a First Step." *Reference Librarian,* no. 11 (fall/winter 1984): 131–145.

This article deals with the problem of defining what a good reference librarian is, determining the behaviors that make up the needed competencies, and then, having determined those, how to evaluate them. As the authors see it, the basic problem is deciding what observable behaviors can provide evidence of achievement. The method suggested, goal analysis, consists of writing down the important goals for reference work and then brainstorming with other knowledgeable individuals in order to select behaviors that a librarian would exhibit if that goal was being met. To avoid the accusation of triviality, each behavior must be carefully assessed according to whether achieving or not achieving it actually has any consequences for library service. The authors further caution readers that the process of goal analysis must necessarily be tied to a unique library setting. Adams and Judd conclude with a helpful case study, showing how this method—which includes a sophisticated tiered approach to allow for varied levels of experience—was actually applied at their college library.

Altman, E., and S. Brown. "What Makes a Librarian Excellent? The View from Phoenix." *Public Libraries* 30 (July/ August 1991): 208–217.

Presents a detailed discussion of a program begun with the goal of challenging public librarians to strive for excellence. Professional staff met to decide which observable behaviors in three major task areas (collection development, reference/reader's advisory services, and community interaction) were indicators of excellence, and how these could be appropriately weighted and measured. After the profile for the "excellent librarian" was established for every area (e.g., adult services, branch heads), librarians evaluated themselves against the new standards. These self-evaluations were reviewed with administrators in order to come up with specific strategies for improvement. Problems encountered (finding sufficient time to do it, documentation) are described, including how the planners attempted to deal with the problems. Staff acceptance of the new system was mixed, and the authors are very honest in providing excerpts of comments, both positive and negative. A complete listing of the profiles for excellence in the three areas is appended, so that a library wishing to do so could easily replicate this program.

Aluri, R. "Improving Reference Service: The Case for Using a Continuous Quality Improvement Method." *RQ* 33 (winter 1993): 220–236.

The author believes that evaluation of reference service is not enough: steps must be taken to improve services on an ongoing basis. He enumerates the variables that affect the success of the reference transaction, in order to make the point that reference librarians alone are not responsible for the success of reference service: many other factors beyond their control are involved. He goes on to explain his reservations about many of the reference studies reported in the literature. Using an analogy from manufacturing, he proposes instead that quality should be built into the transaction from the beginning, rather than wasting time on inspecting the product after it's too late to do anything about it. Key measures for determining the quality of reference service should be identified by the librarians so that service can be monitored (including patron interaction behaviors); then, simple data collection instruments (such as a transaction checksheet) and procedures for collecting data complete the monitoring circle. To avoid having the process turn into peer evaluation, he recommends not identifying the specific librarian involved in the transactions which are recorded for analysis. Once enough data have been collected, identification of problems can begin (several methods of manipulating the data are described). Charts illustrating the use of results are included, but there is no sample of a reference transaction checksheet. Although the methods of data analysis seem rather complicated, the information obtained would seem to be so valuable that it would be worth the effort.

Aluri, R., and M. Reichel. "Performance Evaluation: A Deadly Disease?" *Journal of Academic Librarianship* 20 (July 1994): 145–155.

Basing their remarks on the ideas of W. Edwards Deming, the authors swim against the current in their condemnation of performance appraisal, on the grounds that it creates a climate of fear, stifles teamwork by pitting employees against each other in unhealthy competition, and forces staff to focus on end products rather than on the dynamics of the whole institutional organism. They make some valid points, although I believe there are ways to design performance standards so as to avoid the problems they describe.

American Library Association, RASD Ad Hoc Committee on Behavioral Guidelines for Reference and Information Services. *Guidelines for Behavioral Performance of Reference and Information Services Professionals. RQ*: forthcoming.

This document, while not yet officially published, has been approved by the requisite ALA committees and will appear in a forthcoming issue of *RQ*. It provides excellent descriptions of behaviors expected of reference desk workers, and is highly recommended. As of this writing, it is available on the World Wide Web at http://ala1.ala.org:70/0/alagophxiii/alagophxiiirasd/behavgud.txt

American Library Association, RASD Measurement and Evaluation of Service Committee. "Information Specialists' Use of Machine-Assisted Reference Tools: Evaluation Criteria." *RQ* 31 (fall 1991): 35–38.

Provides a detailed list of objective criteria for use in appraising the skills of online/computer database searchers.

Association of Research Libraries. *Performance Appraisal in Research Libraries*. SPEC Kit 140. Washington, D.C.: Association of Research Libraries, Office of Management Studies, 1988. ED 292 468.

Focusing on professional staff only, this document covers evaluation policies and procedures (including peer review for tenure) used in several ARL libraries, and contains a variety of documents that provide general standards/criteria (not position-specific) for merit review.

Auckland, M. "Training for Staff Appraisal." In *Handbook of Library Training Practice*, vol. 2, ed. R. Prytherch. Aldershot, Hants, England: Gower, 1990.

Reviews the benefits of the recent shift from trait-oriented appraisal to results-oriented evaluations, while stressing that these benefits will be nullified if staff are not trained in conducting appraisals and applying their results effectively. Discusses the two types considered necessary, "knowledge training" and "skills training," giving examples (including a few facsimile documents actually used) of what should be covered and how to do it.

Banks, J. "Motivation and Effective Management of Student Assistants in Academic Libraries." *Journal of Library Administration* 14 (1991) 133–154.

The author quotes data showing that approximately one-fifth of the total workforce in ARL libraries are student assistants; surprisingly, though, a search of the literature indicates that effective management of the work of such a large segment of academic library employees does not appear to be a high priority. This article reports on a literature review on motivation, shelving, and student assistants; gives results of two surveys (one on what other academic libraries were experiencing regarding shelving productivity and what they were using as motivators, and another on student workers' attitudes toward shelving and potential motivators); and describes an experimental incentive program implemented at the author's institution, which was designed to increase student shelver productivity. Although objective performance standards are not discussed per se, there is much useful information here regarding acceptable shelving target figures combined with accuracy expectations.

Barker, L., and S. Enright, "Academic Related Library Staff Appraisal at Imperial College Libraries: A Peer Review Scheme." *British Journal of Academic Librarianship* 8, no. 2 (1993): 113–128.

Describes development and implementation of an elaborate peer appraisal scheme. One has to wonder about the objectivity of these appraisals, since the authors openly acknowledge the fact that the head librarian routinely "draw[s] on her knowledge of the personalities concerned when interpreting the results" of the evaluation of skills. In any event, the goal of the process is merely staff development: the appraisals were deliberately not connected to the library's annual grading and promotion review. Copies of forms (which make the subjective nature of the process quite apparent) are appended.

Beckham, J. "Legally Sound Criteria, Processes and Procedures for the Evaluation of Public School Professional Employees." *Journal of Law and Education* 14 (October 1985): 529–551.

Presents a detailed review of issues as noted in the title, including applicable case law. Although most relevant to school media specialists, much of what is discussed could apply to library personnel in non-school settings as well.

Bender, D. "Improving Personnel Management Through Evaluation." *Library Administration and Management* 8 (spring 1985): 109–112.

Discusses performance evaluation in a very general way, reviewing issues that are common knowledge to anyone who has ever been a supervisor or read anything about it.

Black, W. *Job Analysis in ARL Libraries.* SPEC Kit 135. Washington, D.C.: Association of Research Libraries, Office of Management Studies. ED 285 607.

Most experts agree that one of the first steps in the process of revamping a performance appraisal system is a thorough job analysis. This Spec Kit contains actual forms libraries have used to gather such information from staff.

Brown, J. "Using Quality Concepts to Improve Reference Services. *College and Research Libraries* 55 (May 1994): 211–219.

An academic library reference staff wanted to improve the quality of their service delivery but found little in the literature of practical use, so they also turned to the fields of business and organizational management for help. Using what they learned, they began four projects: a Problem Log, a Suggestion Box, the Wisconsin-Ohio Reference Evaluation Program, and a Reference Automation Quality Circle. In succinct and practical format worthy of emulation by others, the author spells out exactly what they did and what they learned.

Bunge, C. "Evaluating Reference Services and Reference Personnel: Questions and Answers from the Literature." *Reference Librarian*, no. 43 (1994): 195–207.

A bibliographical essay covering 48 citations from the 1980s and 1990s.

Bunge, C. "Gathering and Using Patron and Librarian Perceptions of Question-Answering Success." In *Evaluation of Public Services and Public Services Personnel*, ed. B. Allen, 59–83. Urbana-Champaign, Ill.: University of Illinois, Graduate School of Library and Information Science, 1991.

Describes the Wisconsin-Ohio Reference Evaluation Program. Although the methods used make no attempt to differentiate question-answering ability among specific librarians, this article could be useful if a library director (either academic or public) were inclined to evaluate the reference librarians as a team, rather than as individuals. Copies of all questionnaires used are appended.

Carson, C. "The Development of a Scale to Measure the Self-Efficacy of School Library Media Specialists." *School Library Media Quarterly* 21 (spring 1993): 165–170.

Reviews research studies that relate personal characteristics to success in different roles, and then describes the development and testing of an instrument to predict the success of school librarians in executing behavior needed to produce specified outcomes (according to the theory of Albert Bandura). Subjects responded to 48 statements based on the guidelines contained in *Information Power,* a document produced by AASL and the AECT (ALA, 1988). Although this project has no direct connection to performance evaluation, most of the 48 statements (included in the article) could be adapted to that purpose.

"Changing the Way We Evaluate Employees." *Library Personnel News* 8 (January/February 1994): 4.

Briefly summarizes a presentation at the International Personnel Management Association Conference (Chicago, October 1993) which focused on current trends in performance appraisal, such as (a) evaluation should be used more as a personal development tool than a way of comparing employees, determining merit pay, etc.; (b) better results will be obtained if the appraisal instrument avoids judgmental terms and instead uses phrases emphasizing the frequency of desirable behaviors; and (c) the use of multi-rater, peer, and self-evaluations is increasing.

Chu, F. "Evaluating the Skills of the Systems Librarian." *Journal of Library Administration* 12 (1990): 91–102.

Discusses the problem of defining the job of systems librarian; the problem is that position descriptions not only vary widely among institutions, but they demonstrate that almost anything that has to do with computers may be included—from micros to mainframes. The author reviews the required skills, as identified in a survey of job advertisements, observing that the abilities requested fall into three very disparate groups: planning, installation/implementation, and maintenance. Although to some degree the article reflects the date it was written, and although no specific performance criteria are offered, the detailed review of the complexities of the work of the system librarian (especially in cases where automation has not yet been implemented) would be valuable background reading for anyone trying to write such criteria.

Church, A. "First-Rate Multirater Feedback." *Training* 49 (August 1995): 42–43.

Presents a brief but excellent summary of so-called "360–degree" or "multirater" systems, in which performance evaluation is based on a combination of information obtained from the employee, the supervisor, peers, clients served, etc. Covers the pitfalls, ways to move members of an organization to accept this new approach, and procedures for making use of the feedback for performance improvement.

Cohen, L. "Conducting Performance Evaluations." *Library Trends* 38 (summer 1989): 40–52.

Summarizes a workshop held at the 29th Allerton Institute. The author begins with a short review of common rater biases, and stresses that appraisal systems based on performance goals and measures, not personal traits, avoid this problem. She has adapted the work of S. Creth (*Performance Evaluation: A Goals-Based Approach*, ACRL 1984), presenting it as a practical method for creating performance evaluation procedures that will result in opening the lines of communication between supervisors and employees. The main components (performance planning, monitoring, and evaluation) are described in some detail. This thorough and highly objective approach would provide a good foundation for the overhaul of an existing performance appraisal system.

"Colorado Library Develops Innovative Pay System." *Library Personnel News* 5 (May/June 1991): 5–6.

News of a public library that has eliminated automatic longevity raises, substituting an appraisal system linking objective performance measures to pay increases. Employees are now evaluated in such areas as job knowledge and skill, time utilization, work problems, responsiveness to demands, interpersonal relations, relations with supervisor, practical judgment, orientation to service philosophy, adherence to policy and attendance, communication style with the public and handling of patron inquiries, and management and supervisory behavior. No details on criteria are included, but the program is thought to be so good they have copyrighted it! I haven't seen it, so this isn't an endorsement. Copies may be purchased for $30 from the Pike's Peak Library District, Personnel Department, 5550 N. Union Blvd., Colorado Springs, CO 80918.

Creth, S. *Performance Evaluation: A Goals-Based Approach*. Chicago: Association of College and Research Libraries, 1984.

Continuing education workbook designed to help supervisors become better evaluators. Presents the principles of writing concrete goals and objectives for employee performance and preparing for/conducting the evaluation interview.

Creth, S. "Personnel Issues for Academic Librarians: A Review and Perspectives for the Future." *College and Research Libraries* 50 (March 1989): 144–152.

This is a fascinating historical perspective on the continuing debate over whether librarianship really *is* a profession, the appropriateness of faculty status for academic librarians, and indications of some directions that librarianship could take in the future to break out of the confining bureaucratic structure which has heretofore hindered librarians from attaining true professional status. Contains no specific information about performance expectations.

Cullen, R. "Evaluation and Performance Measurement in Reference Services." *New Zealand Libraries* 47 (March 1992): 11–15.

The author recommends routine use of a reference transaction record (sample not included) as one way of gathering more useful evaluative information about reference service than mere statistical measures can provide. Suggests and briefly discusses basic areas affecting the quality of reference service that should be evaluated in all libraries: the collection, the physical environment, and staff skills.

Cullen, R., and G. Austen. "Performance Appraisal." *Australian Academic and Research Libraries* 18 (March 1987): 35–40.

Prior to developing a new comprehensive staff development program for the authors' own academic library, a survey of other Australian academic libraries was conducted in order to get information regarding their practices and attitudes toward staff appraisal. The study revealed that 68% did not have a performance evaluation system at all. Of those that did have one, 31% reported some staff resistance to appraisal, and nearly 70% indicated that staff were not evaluated against a standard, but only according to whether they were working to the best of their ability.

Cummins, T. "Personnel Management in Libraries." *Public Library Quarterly* 10 (1990): 25–44.

Presents a review of the literature of personnel management in libraries through 1985, with brief summaries of findings under the following categories: purposes of performance evaluation, appraisers of performance, users of evaluations, when to evaluate, appraisal methods, and staff development.

Cummins, T., and M. Carden. "Productivity Efforts in Public Libraries." *Public Libraries* 26 (Winter 1987): 140–142.

Describes how the evaluative framework suggested by Dougherty and Heinritz in *Scientific Management of Library Operations* (1982) could be applied to productivity measurement in public libraries; addresses quantity output measurement techniques for the concrete production-related aspects of library work, but does not deal with the problem of assessing quality of output.

Dougherty, R., and F. Heinritz. *Scientific Management of Library Operations*. Metuchen, N.J.: Scarecrow Press, 1982.

Chapter 12 contains detailed information on a method for

deriving performance standards; the results of its application to the clerical tasks of acquisitions is provided. Although the authors freely admit that it would probably be difficult to apply the same process to professional work (because it is generally not production-oriented), this is still well worth looking at.

Duncan, D. "Performance Appraisal: Reducing Rating Errors at Pensacola Junior College." *CUPA Journal* 39 (winter 1988): 40–54.

Reports a research project on how supervisors are influenced by the design of evaluation forms. The project was initiated by Duncan in response to the problem of consistently inflated ratings of employees. He theorized that the problem was caused by a form that did not allow supervisors to distinguish between standards and work behavior; the items on which employees were evaluated and the phrases from which evaluators had to select, were more descriptive of personality than performance. The new form he designed and tested resulted in scores that conformed to a normal curve, and were thus presumably more accurate. Samples of both the old and new forms are included.

Durey, P. "The Appraisal and Professional Development of Staff in Academic Libraries." *New Zealand Libraries* 46 (March 1991): 7–9.

A broad comparison of appraisal and staff development procedures in New Zealand and the United States, Britain, and Sweden. At the author's university, appraisal is clearly separated from merit pay, and, at staff insistence, it is used strictly for professional development purposes.

Eyres, P. "Legally Defensible Performance Appraisal Systems." *Personnel Journal* 68 (July 1989): 58–62.

The title of the article says it all, plus it's concise, practical, and right to the point. The author (an attorney) closes with a checklist for managers which should be read by all supervisors.

Farah, B. "Academic Reference Librarians: A Case for Self-Evaluation." *Reference Librarian*, no. 25–26 (1989): 495–505.

Presents a helpful framework for the needed redefinition of performance standards for academic reference librarians; makes the point that the demands being made on these librarians are changing rapidly, and that their traditional metaphorical and physical tie to a "reference desk" limits their abilities to respond to new needs. The best way for administrators to grasp what these changes are and to plan how to meet them is to ask those who are actually trying to provide the expected services to identify the tasks they are now fulfilling. Includes a literature review on the functions and future of reference service.

Farmer, J. "Performance Related Pay for Librarians: An Overview." *Personnel Training and Education* 9, no. 2 (1992): 53–57.

Reviews the historical background of the development of performance-based pay systems, noting that there is no evidence to suggest that such strategies are either appropriate or effective within librarianship, since creating measurable criteria for public service work is so difficult—perhaps impossible. Concerns are also expressed about the competitiveness problem which inevitably arises when employees are rated against each other. The author concludes that much more investigation is needed before pay-for-performance schemes are implemented in libraries.

Farmer, L., and S. Johnson. "Evaluation Portfolios: Evidence of Effectiveness." *Book Report* 10 (March/April 1992): 21–22.

Provides helpful information on the use of portfolios (collections of materials that document an individual's efforts, progress, accomplishments, etc.) in the evaluation of school librarians, plus a lengthy list of examples of items that could be included. Also contains recommendations on effective presentation formats.

Fletcher, C. "Appraisal: An Idea Whose Time Has Gone?" *Personnel Management* 4 (September 1993): 34–37.

Briefly reviews recent trends in performance evaluation resulting from the changing fashions in human resource management, such as TQM, the competency movement, performance management, peer/upward appraisal, etc.

Frick, E. "Qualitative Evaluation of User Education Programs: The Best Choice?" *Research Strategies* 8 (winter 1990): 4–13.

Presents a thorough explanation of qualitative vs. quantitative evaluation and how to decide which method is best in a given situation, i.e., user education. Does not get into the specifics of actually conducting a qualitative evaluation.

Fuller, F. "Evaluating Student Assistants as Library Employees." *College and Research Libraries News* 52 (January 1990): 11–13.

The author takes as a given that it is difficult to determine with any precision the degree to which employees are fulfilling job requirements, especially student workers. Therefore, the emphasis is placed more on developing personal work habits in library aides, rather than truly measuring performance. Although no sample of the evaluation form is included, the description provided leads one to conclude that the criteria used are somewhat subjective.

Gorman, K. *Performance Evaluation in Reference Services in ARL Libraries.* SPEC Kit 139. Washington D.C: Association of Research Libraries, Office of Management Studies, 1987. ED 289 525.

Reports results of two surveys (1986: collection and use of reference statistics, and 1987: qualitative measures of reference service), including a discussion of trends and issues in reference service evaluation. As usual with the SPEC Kit series, the best part is the collection of documents submitted from the surveyed libraries; lots of good material here.

Green, A. "Staff Appraisal or Development Review: A New Zealand Journey." *Personnel Training and Education* 9, no. 2 (1992): 39–43.

Includes descriptions of widely varied appraisal procedures at three university libraries and the National Library, followed by the author's evaluation of the effectiveness and staff acceptance of the different schemes used. Provides few details on what is evaluated, and the ones that are supplied appear to be fairly subjective.

Green, A. "A Survey of Staff Appraisal in University Libraries." *British Journal of Academic Librarianship* 8, no. 3 (1993): 193–209.

An insight into the author's personal attitude toward performance evaluation is contained in his opening remark on the confluence of the American inventions of the H-bomb and staff appraisal, both of which emerged at the time of WWII. The study reveals the slow acceptance of performance evaluation in British libraries: over 80% of those surveyed had not introduced appraisals until 1990–91, while another 9.6% had not started staff evaluations until 1992–93. The majority expressed a positive attitude toward appraisals, despite the fact that 40% reported that the library staff did not take them very seriously. The most interesting parts of the article are the two anonymous case studies, which document the history, development, and results of the implementation of performance appraisal in two academic libraries.

Gross, M., and E. Young. "Planning and Conducting the Performance Appraisal Conference in a Library Setting." *Behavioral and Social Sciences Librarian* 12 (1993): 21–43.

Begins with a brief history of the development of employee performance appraisal, then discusses the negative aspects of the appraisal interview. A variety of standard techniques for maximizing appraisal interviewing effectiveness are listed and described. A 13-page annotated bibliography of articles and books dealing with performance review (including non-library examples) is appended.

Halachmi, A. "From Performance Appraisal to Performance Targeting." *Public Personnel Management* 22 (summer 1993): 323–344.

The author explains in detail why he believes that performance appraisal, which evaluates past activity, is an expensive waste of time and may even hurt future job performance. He advocates the substitution of performance targeting, a joint effort by both supervisor and subordinate to determine what needs to be done in order to meet organizational goals, what the employee could contribute to that effort, and what the supervisor must do to create the environment in which the employee's contribution can be maximized. Sounds good in theory, but, since even the author admits that a review must still be conducted periodically to determine whether the employee met the targets, what's the point? Seems like we're right back where we started.

Hannabuss, S. "Analysing Appraisal Interviews." *Scottish Libraries*, no. 30 (November/December 1991): 13–15.

The author presents and explains a form designed to allow supervisors and their subordinates to evaluate each other on how the performance appraisal interview was handled. Those who work in the typical fast-paced library environment would probably judge this exercise to be an impractical luxury if done regularly; on the other hand, the questionnaire would certainly elicit some interesting information that could lead to greater self-knowledge on both sides.

Hannabuss, S. "The Importance of Performance Measures." *Library Review* 36 (winter 1987): 248–253.

Offers a very general discussion of what performance standards are and their value as managerial tools within a library. While admitting the inadequacies inherent in the use of quantitative standards, they are nevertheless recommended as simple decision-making instruments; some examples of ways in which library data can be statistically manipulated are described. No information on quality measures or standards for individual staff members is included.

Hanneken, H., et al. *Staffing Your Library/Media Center.* Springfield, Ill.: Illinois State Board of Education, 1979. ED 216 677.

Provides detailed lists of tasks expected of media specialists and their support staff.

Hansel, P. "Quantity Is Not Necessarily Quality: A Challenge to Librarians to Develop Meaningful Standards of Performance for Library Reference Services." *North Carolina Libraries* 48 (fall 1990): 184–187.

The author urges libraries to get away from strictly quantitative measures of reference service (i.e., counting questions) and admit that the number of questions answered says nothing about the quality of the service being offered. She makes the interesting point that a large number of questions *could* simply mean that (among many other possibilities) the library is so unorganized that users cannot find things on their own! She reviews past research on the disappointing results of unobtrusive testing of reference service, and counters the accusation sometimes made that this type of research is unethical, by stating that it is even more unethical to advertise a service of questionable quality. She reports on her library's successful use of the Wisconsin-Ohio Reference Evaluation Project forms and recommends another unobtrusive evaluation project conducted in Maryland by Ralph Gers and Lillie Seward (Gers is available as a consultant for libraries that want to replicate the program). She ends with an exhortation to libraries to consider that in many libraries today reference librarians are overwhelmed by their workload and are simply being asked to do too much.

Hansel, P. "Unobtrusive Evaluation: An Administrative Learning Experience." *Reference Librarian*, no. 19 (1987): 315–325.

The author shares what was learned from her public library system's study of information service delivery, which was prompted by the realization that the institution did not have adequate performance standards in place to allow them to deal with a problem employee. Although a review of the literature made it seem that the unobtrusive observation method might be too difficult or costly, they decided to try it anyway to get the most accurate picture of service quality. The study was successful, and revealed that paraprofessional staff in the branches were doing well, within the limitations of available resources; that it was sometimes difficult for patrons to contact specific staff members to whom they were referred; that suspected problem performers were indeed inadequate (but so were some of the staff "stars"); that patrons have lower expectations of library service than the librarians do; and that accuracy of responses to questions is indeed too low (confirming what has been reported in many previous studies). To help address some of the problems identified, the library instituted a series of regular reference training sessions and took steps to see that procedures for delivery of updated materials to branches were followed. (Samples of the questions used in the survey were not included.)

Harrison, C. "Quality in Learning Support Services." *Law Librarian* 25 (December 1994): 212–215.

This somewhat theoretical article concerns the need to establish documentary evidence of quality in library service delivery, which the author maintains can only occur if the following factors exist within the institutional structure: a focus on human resources and staff development, a review process for information delivery (designed with the assistance of a quality development specialist), and a feedback system. To achieve quality, each department should have its own mission statement, derived from that of the institution, including clear goals and objectives. Once these are in place, a development plan can be implemented to measure reliability, accountability, responsiveness, and proactivity (some details on exactly what these categories mean, and examples of what could be measured are included). The indicators mentioned, however, are the usual ones (e.g., number of students and staff, number of books per student, number of ILLs) which really are about quantity, not quality.

Hartzell, G. "Letting Others Know How They're Doing: Performance Appraisal Conferences for School Library Workers." *Book Report* 12 (September/October 1993): 15–17, 20.

Offers sensible advice on how to prepare for and conduct the appraisal interview.

Hatcher, K. "The Role of the Systems Librarian/Administrator: A Report of the Survey." *Library Administration and Management* 9 (spring 1995): 106–109.

While not as useful as the B. Leonard article cited below, this report does offer a few additional details on the tasks expected of a systems librarian, as determined through analysis of a 1991 survey of academic libraries.

Haycock, K. "Evaluation of the Teacher-Librarian: A Discussion Guide." *Emergency Librarian* 18 (January/February 1991): 15–18, 21–22.

The author sets out to help both principals who may be uncertain about the appropriate criteria for evaluating school librarians, and teacher-librarians who are concerned that their job descriptions are so broad that it would be impossible for one person to do it all. He gives some sound and practical advice for both, then offers an excellent outline for evaluation of the teacher-librarian in nine areas of competence, with a list of specific criteria for each area.

Hook, P. "Another 'Home-Grown' Evaluation Instrument." *Book Report* 10 (March/April 1992): 19–20.

When librarians in the Fairfax, Va., school system learned that they were not to be part of a new evaluation process for teachers, they decided to campaign for inclusion. Once they were accepted, the guidelines previously written to apply to classroom teachers were suitably modified, and an evaluation cycle including announced and unannounced observations (some of which are done by peers) was established. At the end of each year, all the observation reports are collated and used by the principal to assign a rating, which is then used for assignment to an intervention program, for termination, or for merit pay. Includes a list of standards (which are quite rigorous), plus samples of the observable behaviors.

Hults, P. "Reference Evaluation: An Overview." *Reference Librarian*, no. 38 (1992): 141–150.

Presents a historical overview of the rise of interest in reference quality evaluation, which the author traces back to the unobtrusive observation studies begun during the early 1970s; prior to that, evaluation was almost exclusively quantitative. General guidelines are offered on what must be considered before a reference evaluation program is begun, and the need to take action on evaluation results is stressed.

Isbell, D., and L. Kammerlocher. "A Formative, Collegial Approach to Evaluating Course-Integrated Instruction. *Research Strategies* 12 (winter 1994): 24–32.

Although this article is not oriented toward performance standards per se, some of the material included in the university-level BI evaluation program described can help in identifying behavioral elements that define the successful provider of bibliographic instruction.

Jenkins, B., and M. Smalls. *Performance Appraisal in Academic Libraries.* CLIP Note 12. Chicago: Association of College and Research Libraries, 1990.

Reproduces 16 mostly trait-oriented appraisal documents (both professional and paraprofessional) from 11 college libraries.

Johnson, D. "At the Ends of Our Job: Using Planning and Reporting to Build Program Support." *Book Report* 10 (March/April 1992): 24–25.

The author (a high school librarian) stresses the importance of written goals and objectives, and describes how to construct them. He also explains the use of these planning documents in his annual performance review, and how he further strengthens awareness of media center activities through strategic dissemination of information in a wide variety of ways.

Jones, L. "Making Sense of the Annual Performance Review." *Colorado Libraries* 18 (March 1992): 31–32.

Presents general thoughts on the problems of doing performance assessment, plus some hints on making the evaluation process both more valuable and less stressful for employees, supervisors, and institutions.

Jordan, P. "Library Performers: Groups and Individuals." *British Journal of Academic Librarianship,* 7, no. 3 (1992): 177–185.

Proposes that, since librarians seldom work in isolation, the assessment of the performance of work groups is just as important as evaluation of individuals. The actual implementation as described is a disappointment, however, since it seems mainly to consist of a group meeting to elaborate verbally on the annual report. Closes with some remarks on the problems associated with individual appraisals, and how some of these might be alleviated.

Kaehr, R. "Personnel Appraisal, Who Needs It?" *Journal of Academic Librarianship* 16 (March 1990): 35–36.

Serves as a meditation on the importance and use of performance appraisal. Includes a review of a few opinions on the subject drawn from library literature. Also includes the author's comments on some of the implications of these ideas.

Kathman, J., and M. Kathman. "Performance Measures for Student Assistants."*College and Research Libraries* 53 (July 1992): 299–304.

When the Kathmans observed that there was nothing in the literature dealing with overall performance measures for student workers in academic libraries, and that evaluation schemes proposed for full-time employees are not always appropriate to part-time student staff (who have no long-term commitment to the job), they decided to give some much-needed attention to this neglected area. They first discuss the need for evaluation of student work and flexibility in standard-setting, then offer some general guidelines and procedures for how such evaluation could be accomplished.

Kemp, J. "Reevaluating Support Staff Positions." *Library Administration and Management* 9 (winter 1995): 37–43.

Because automation was perceived to have changed some paraprofessional jobs substantially, this academic library thoroughly reviewed all of them; one result was the upgrade of one-third of the positions. Includes detailed description of the steps in the review process, the timetable, and the problems encountered. A copy of the Position Description Questionnaire used to solicit information for job analysis is appended.

Kendrick, C. "Performance Measures of Shelving Accuracy." *Journal of Academic Librarianship* 17 (March 1991): 16–18.

Back to the basics: Kendrick quotes Flexner's 1927 observation that libraries are only useful to the extent that the materials can be easily located! He defines and briefly discusses the concept of performance measurement, then describes the quality control program for shelving developed and implemented at SUNY Stony Brook Library. Under this system, shelving accuracy of 91% was attained, which compared favorably to the few other institutions that have tried something similar and reported results. The author also surveyed other SUNY libraries to learn if/how others were dealing with evaluation of shelving accuracy. Although the process used is somewhat labor-intensive, it seems simple and practical enough to be applied in most libraries.

King, G. "Performance Appraisal in the Automated Environment." *Journal of Library Administration* 13 (1990): 195–204.

Recognizing that library work has changed considerably since the advent of computers, and that many more jobs are now done in the context of teams, the author outlines steps that can be used to develop a performance appraisal scheme to fit a specific library situation. She proceeds on the assumption that most libraries will be using such a system for individual development, rather than awarding merit pay. Basic components of any appraisal system are listed, with some attention given to automation as a factor. Specific performance criteria are not within the scope of this article.

King, G., and S. Mahmoodi. "Peer Performance Appraisal of Reference Librarians in a Public Library." In *Evaluation of Public Services and Public Services Personnel*, ed. B. Allen, 167–203. Urbana-Champaign, Ill.: University of Illinois Graduate School of Library and Information Science, 1991.

After gradually (over a 10-year period) moving away from a traditional hierarchical management structure to a team approach, members of a public library reference department initiated a successful peer/team/project performance appraisal system. The system itself is described in considerable detail (including the problem-solving techniques used in order to maintain momentum, and the process of expanding the system beyond the original group that established it). Five years afterward, the program is still in use and results have been very positive.

Kleiner, J. "Ensuring Quality Reference Desk Service: The Introduction of a Peer Process." *RQ* 30 (spring 1991): 349–361.

Briefly summarizes the history of performance appraisal both in the United States and at Louisiana State University Libraries, then describes LSU's successful introduction of formative peer evaluation for reference staff. Their "Recommended Desk Review Checklist" is appended, but not a full copy of the peer review document itself.

Koch, H. "Criteria-Based Performance Evaluations for Hospital Library Managers." *Special Libraries* 80 (fall 1989): 269–271.

The Joint Commission of Accreditation of Healthcare Organizations now requires health care institutions to use specific, criteria-based evaluations for measurement of employee performance, making it necessary to revise standards for hospital librarians; this article describes how this was done at a hospital in Michigan. A complete copy of the position description and corresponding performance evaluation document is appended.

Krull, J. "A Merit Pay Plan for Public Libraries." *Library Journal* 112 (June 15, 1987): 34–37.

Offers a practical approach to establishing a merit pay plan, including descriptions of the following steps: developing a classification scheme based on detailed job descriptions and grouping according to levels of responsibility/difficulty; determining salary ranges appropriate to each level; implementing a merit pay plan based only on performance evaluations (without automatic step or cost-of-living increases); and determining the increases to be associated with each degree or range of performance ratings. Although the author stresses the importance of having an objective appraisal system, which results in accurate performance ratings for each individual so that merit pay can be allocated equitably, he does not address methods of developing such a system.

Lancaster, F. "Evaluation As a Management Tool." *Public Libraries* 29 (September/October 1990): 289–294.

Deals with the practical uses of evaluation of services (not personnel), in order to control costs and determine the effectiveness, benefits, and cost-effectiveness of library efforts.

Lancaster, F., C. Elzy, and A. Nourie. "The Diagnostic Evaluation of Reference Service in an Academic Library." In

Evaluation of Public Services and Public Services Personnel, ed. B. Allen, 43–57. Urbana-Champaign, Ill.: University of Illinois Graduate School of Library and Information Science, 1991.

Presents a very interesting report of a project conducted in 1989, involving the unobtrusive evaluation of reference librarians at Illinois State University. The authors suggest that results could be used as part of the justification for awarding/withholding merit increases; this method of study, which is often resented by the subjects once they know about it, is defended on the grounds that teaching faculty are regularly subjected to anonymous evaluation by students. Enough details of the process are given to allow for local replication if desired.

Larson, C., and L. Dickson, "Developing Behavioral Reference Desk Performance Standards." *RQ* 33 (spring 1994): 349–357.

The authors try to fill a perceived gap in library literature by focusing on the formation of standards based on objective, observable criteria applied to individuals, rather than whole departments. Not surprisingly, they report that they found little of practical use in the literature, but they do provide succinct annotations for the articles they read prior to beginning work on their own standards. The entire reference department (a mix of professionals and paraprofessionals) first met to work out a shared understanding of what ideal reference service based on behavior would look like. Broad goals with lists of desired related behaviors were developed. Initially the intention was to use these within the context of peer review, but well-grounded fears of a negative outcome caused that approach to be postponed. Instead, the behavioral standards have been used for supervisory evaluation and for training new staff. Both the "raw data" originally produced in staff meetings and the final evaluation criteria are appended. Put this one near the top of your must-read list.

Leach, R. "Developing Performance Standards for Library Staff." In *Library Serials Standards: Development, Implementation, Impact*. Proceedings of the Third Annual Serials Conference. Westport, Conn.: Meckler, 1984.

Begins by defining the major reasons for being concerned about performance standards (size of personnel expenditures, need for accountability, ease of acquiring productivity data with the advent of automation, and a desire to increase the effectiveness of employee evaluation), then describes in considerable detail exactly what performance standards *are*, and the process of development and implementation. The author does an excellent job of explaining the possible pitfalls and making clear the difference between the usual employee appraisal and the one based on objective results. Two responses follow, dealing in a more practical (but brief) way with the difficulties encountered when performance standards systems were implemented in specific institutions.

Leonard, B. "The Role of the Systems Librarian/Administrator: A Preliminary Report." *Library Administration and Management* 7 (spring 1993): 113–116.

This is the initial report of a survey of academic libraries conducted for the purpose of defining the responsibilities and organizational placement of the systems librarian. Includes three useful charts derived from the results: duties and responsibilities, knowledge level required, and skill level required.

Lindsey, J. *Performance Evaluation: A Management Basic for Librarians*. Phoenix, Ariz.: Oryx Press, 1986.

These readings cover all aspects of performance appraisal. Very little is relevant to our purposes here, except for a behavioral observation rating scale for technical services personnel.

Lofgren, H. "Priority and Performance Evaluation: A Tool for Libraries." *Australian Library Journal* 41 (February 1992): 14–30.

Presents the outcomes of a research project on critical success factor analysis (the identification of factors of particular importance to the success of individuals, departments, institutions, etc.). The author explains the critical success factor approach and grounds it in the literature, then shows how the methodology was applied to Australian libraries through studies conducted with librarians and other information professionals. This type of analysis allows library managers not only to identify areas crucial to institutional success, but also to gauge the potential cost-effectiveness of resources invested in those areas as compared to their impact on success. Although the goal of this research was to apply the critical success factors method to the organization, it seems that this method could be used equally well in the development of such criteria for individuals. Very interesting.

Lupone, G., and B. Trizzino. "Performance Standards for Library Support Staff." *Library Personnel News* 3 (summer 1989): 45–46.

Offers a very brief account of the process of developing behaviorally based standards for paraprofessional staff in an academic library.

McClure, C. "Output Measures, Unobtrusive Testing, and Assessing the Quality of Reference Services." *Reference Librarian* (fall/winter 1984): 215–233.

The author discusses the importance of output measures and unobtrusive testing, their implementation, and use in formal planning. He also suggests (and explains how to calculate) such measures such as correct answer fill rate, correct answers per reference staff hour, and reference services delivery rate. He recommends against trying to use these strategies to evaluate individual performance.

McDonagh, B. "Appraising Appraisals." *Law Librarian* 26 (September 1995): 423–425.

Presents a very general discussion of the benefits of performance appraisal and outlines the benefits of different methods. Probably nothing you haven't heard before.

MacDougall, A. "Performance Assessment: Today's Confusion, Tomorrow's Solution?" *IFLA Journal* 17, no. 4 (1991): 371–378.

Noting the increasing attention that accountability has been receiving worldwide, the author proposes that the ability to assess institutional performance effectively is a managerial technique that information professionals are expected to have in order to be judged excellent employees themselves. His review of the literature leads him to conclude that, so far, the practical has been emphasized over the theoretical, and that although the subject is gaining increased notice in the literature, the majority of librarians are probably not deeply committed to it. In his view, part of the problem is widespread confusion over terminology (complicated by linguistic differences among countries), how to apply the various theories of performance, and why such application is necessary. He mentions a few recent

American and British publications that provide library output measures and briefly discusses some efforts to apply performance assessment at the international level.

McElroy, R. "Standards and Guidelines in Performance Measurement." *British Journal of Academic Librarianship* 4, no. 2 (1989): 88–98.

The author states at the outset that he will not offer definitive methods of measuring performance; instead, his aim is to consider whether published standards and guidelines can be helpful to such efforts. He cautions libraries to avoid getting caught up in quantity measurements to the degree that they lose sight of quality, and urges managers to have confidence in their own judgment. In the past, he notes, national and association standards seemed to presume that more is better (and so they dealt almost exclusively with enumeration of quantities); recent efforts have been more sophisticated, and he briefly mentions several British standards/guidelines documents, and their possible use as a means to persuade college/university administrators that improvement is needed. He anticipates changes in future standards documents, such that they will be even more understandable and acceptable to non-library managers, and he urges librarians to cooperate with such movements so that they can begin to talk the same language as the academic administrators who must make funding decisions for their libraries.

Mann, C. "Grow Your Own: Creating and Installing an Evaluation Instrument for Librarians." *Book Report* 10 (March/April 1992): 17–20.

The author's school system decided to address and correct the problem of trying to use a state-sanctioned appraisal instrument—designed for teachers—to evaluate media specialists. To that end, a committee of elementary and secondary librarians developed a list of ways in which the performance of media specialists could be observed, examples of criteria that could be used as indicators of performance, and explanations of these indicators for principals who might not be very familiar with library practice. Before it was put into use, training sessions were conducted for administrators (format/content of these sessions is described). A one-page sample of the new Evaluation Instrument is included, plus suggestions to help facilitate replication of their process in your own organization. Very practical and informative.

Martin, S. "The Role of the Systems Librarian." *Journal of Library Administration* 9, no. 4 (1988): 57–68.

Written in the relatively early days of library automation, this article describes the qualifications needed for a systems librarian, and what one actually does (or should be expected to do). The general task categories presented provide an excellent basis on which either to write a job description or develop performance criteria for this position.

Meyer, L., and R. Wood. *Library Staff Evaluations and Merit Pay Decisions: A Case Study*. Huntsville, Tex.: Sam Houston State University, 1992. ED 344 606.

Provides detailed information about the process used by an academic library staff to totally revamp their evaluation system, primarily in order to ensure that criteria used for annual personnel evaluation and criteria used for awarding merit pay were the same. The new forms devised include a section containing job criteria applicable to all staff, a second part in which only job-specific criteria are rated, and a third segment in which staff record their accomplishments, committee work, training/workshops, etc. A weighting system was used to ensure that each criterion, when evaluated, had reasonable correspondence to its importance in each particular individual's job. A survey to assess staff reaction was conducted after the new system was implemented, and most responses were positive. Includes copies of both the old and new evaluation forms.

Mohrman, A., S. Resnick-West, and E. Lawler III. *Designing Performance Appraisal Systems.* San Francisco: Jossey-Bass, 1989.

Contains specific guidelines for development and implementation of a new evaluation system, including case studies, a review and pros and cons of various appraisal methods, potential sources of appraisal feedback, and legal considerations. Although the book is geared to the corporate world, it is very readable and offers lots of practical advice for those setting out to revamp their library's evaluation system.

Morris, B. "Performance Appraisal: Getting the Most Out of People." *State Librarian* 37 (March 1989): 9–10.

Presents the text of a brief talk given at a conference, designed to convince listeners of the importance of appraisal and provide some general ideas that should be considered prior to developing a new system.

Naylor, A., and K. Jenkins. "An Investigation of Principals' Perceptions of Library Media Specialists' Performance Evaluation Terminology." *School Library Media Quarterly* 16 (summer 1988): 234–243.

North Carolina school librarians were fearful of a new state-mandated evaluation system, which they felt would result in their being judged by persons inadequately informed about library media center operations—thus this study. The research showed that although principals had a very high regard for the technological skills of the media specialists, they did indeed lack technical knowledge of media center operations. Copies of the first and revised versions of the media coordinator performance appraisal instruments are appended.

Olson, L. "Reference Service Evaluation in Medium-Sized Academic Libraries: A Model." *Journal of Academic Librarianship* 9 (January 1984): 322–329.

Urges libraries not to use the perceived "unquantifiable" nature of reference service as an excuse for avoiding appraisal; although lack of national quality standards is indeed a problem, the information product and instruction in the use of resources delivered at the reference desk can and should be evaluated. Some specific objectives that could be applied to a program of reference evaluation (on a departmental level) are described, including anticipation of possible pitfalls and examples of actual questions that could be used in an unobtrusive test. A Reference Service Questionnaire for patrons who have just completed a transaction with a reference librarian, plus scoring/evaluation criteria are reproduced within the article text.

Pawlowski, C. "Library Media Paraprofessionals: We Can't Live Without Them!" *Book Report* 12 (September 1993): 19–20.

Offers a very specific list of tasks and expectations for the media center assistant in four categories—clerical, technical, instructional, and promotional (i.e., PR activities)—and good suggestions on how to conduct effective evaluations.

Perkins, G. "Enhancement of Organizational Structure Through Upward Evaluation." *Library Administration and Management* 6 (fall 1992): 198–202.

Presents review of the literature on evaluation of supervisors by their subordinates, and a preliminary report of research on implementation of upward evaluation at an academic library. Job analysis was used to develop the questionnaire, which was reviewed and edited both by the supervisor and supervisees; based on this review, about one third of the areas identified under job responsibilities were eliminated, because the supervisees did not feel qualified to evaluate them. Particular attention was given to rater anonymity, which was felt to be essential; the supervisor who was rated had generally favorable comments about the process and its outcomes (which were developmental only, and not part of the regular personnel review cycle). Unfortunately, a copy of the evaluation instrument was not included.

Perkins, G. "Positive Outcomes of Behaviorally Based Performance Measurement: A Review Article."*Library Administration and Management* 5 (winter 1991): 45–48.

This bibliographical essay covers both library literature and materials from the fields of industrial psychology and business. Along the way, quite a bit of explanation of behaviorally based performance evaluation and its benefits, uses, and measurement is provided. This would be a good article to use if you need to convince others of the advantages of reforming your performance appraisal system.

Perkins, G. "The Value of Upward Evaluation in Libraries: Part II." *Library Administration and Management* 9 (Summer 1995): 166–175.

Following up on her first piece on the subject of employee evaluation of supervisors, Perkins focuses on the supervisors' acceptance of this feedback, and reviews research on the results of upward evaluation in both librarianship and the fields of business and industrial psychology. She then describes in detail the process followed at Western Kentucky University, which resulted in the development and implementation of a successful supervisor evaluation protocol. Both the research and the author's experience at her institution suggest that such evaluations are useful to supervisors and result in positive changes in behavior.

Pinkston, J. "Assessment and Accountability at Toledo-Lucas County Public Library." *Reference Librarian*, no. 38 (1992): 41–52.

An account of how a public library has tried to monitor its effectiveness continually with user surveys, use statistics, and close community contact, and how it has attempted to anticipate and meet local needs, particularly in the area of economic development.

Posnett, N. W. "Introduction of Performance Indicators at the Institute of Development Studies." *Journal of Information Science* 19, no. 5 (1993): 377–387.

Describes the implementation of a system to monitor performance, efficiency, and effectiveness of a special library (the institution itself, not its personnel). To minimize the impact on the staff, outside consultants were initially employed to assist the administration in selecting the indicators to be measured (the main focus was cost-effectiveness). Eventually, however, these indicators had to be fine-tuned by staff more familiar with the actual work. Furthermore, the time needed to collect data was found to be much greater than anticipated; for this reason, some of the consultants' recommendations were rejected. A total of 14 indicators were selected, and these are listed and their scope briefly explained.

Pritchard, S. "Determining Quality in Academic Libraries." *Library Trends* 44 (January 1996): 572–594.

Summarizes attempts to measure service quality in academic libraries, from traditional methods, to TQM, to more modern, user-defined criteria. Includes discussion on how quality measures in academic libraries must be linked to educational outcomes.

Quinn, B. "Beyond Efficacy: The Exemplar Librarian As a New Approach to Reference Evaluation." *Illinois Libraries* 76 (summer 1994): 163–173.

Seeking to help us escape from the prison of mere "effectiveness," this author instead asks the question, "What makes a reference librarian great?" His research method was to post a query on several listservs, asking librarians to send in anecdotes about the best reference librarian they'd ever met, and why he or she was outstanding. Content analysis of the responses resulted in the production of a list of 22 characteristics that "great" reference librarians exhibited. Many direct quotes from the respondents are included to illustrate the characteristics. This article is not only practical and thought-provoking but also very inspiring; it should be read by every reference librarian.

Ray, T., and P. Hawthorne. *Librarian Job Descriptions in ARL Libraries.* SPEC Kit 194. Washington, D.C.: Association of Research Libraries, Office of Management Services, 1993: ED 364 231.

As the title indicates, includes a fairly wide selection of professional job/position descriptions (including some forms to be used for job analysis) from several large academic libraries.

Reed, D. "Management in Context: Making the Concepts Real." *Kentucky Libraries* 59 (winter 1995): 28–30.

While acknowledging Deming's condemnation of performance appraisals—especially when linked to annual salaries—Reed nevertheless maintains that the problem is not evaluation itself, but the kinds of evaluations used in many public sector organizations, many of which use one-size-fits-all forms for everyone no matter what the job is. He also believes that the implicit assumption that everyone's scores will fall into a normal curve is very damaging: he cites Handly's concept of *assumption of competence* as an idea on which to found an evaluation system that would ultimately lead to higher morale in organizations.

Robbins-Carter, J., and D. Zweizig. "Evaluating Library Personnel; Are We There Yet?" Part 5. *American Libraries* 17 (February 1986): 108+

Outlines the basic problems of personnel appraisal, and recommends an MBO (management by objective) process. The method is described, but no examples are given.

Rubin, R. "The Development of a Performance Evaluation Instrument for Upward Evaluation of Supervisors by Subordinates." *Library and Information Science Research* 16 (fall 1994): 315–328.

The literature of management suggests that performance evaluations should include data from as many sources as possible, leading to the conclusion that appraisal from the subordinates of a supervisor would be useful. Since such a process has the potential to do harm, however, this process must be pursued with caution, using only valid evaluation instruments. The author's public library decided to create such an instrument. The methods and process are outlined and an extensive list of evaluation statements generated by staff is included, as well as a copy of the final Supervisory Evaluation Form. Statistical analysis was performed to determine reliability (which was high).

Rubin, R. "Evaluation of Reference Personnel." In *Evaluation of Public Services and Public Services Personnel*, ed. B. Allen, 147–165. Urbana-Champaign, Ill.: University of Illinois, Graduate School of Library and Information Science, 1991.

Offers a very general introduction to evaluation. Focuses on rating errors and their causes, also describes and gives brief examples of various types of rating systems: trait-anchored, behaviorally based, goal-oriented.

Ryans, C. "Insights into Performance Evaluations for Library Directors." *Catholic Library World* 61 (March/April 1990): 207–211, 226.

This is a subject seldom touched on: performance evaluation of the director. Ryans suggests that library staff (as well as higher level administrators and others outside the library who have worked with the individual) should be involved. She recommends beginning with a self-assessment, followed by a survey of those whose input into the appraisal is sought (questions can be developed through a review of the library's mission statement). A very useful table of suggested survey questions is appended.

Schabo, P., and D. Baculis. "Speed and Accuracy for Shelving." *Library Journal* 114 (October 1, 1989): 67–68.

A public library addresses the problem of motivating part-time workers hired to perform the boring task of reshelving materials accurately. Library pages are required to keep track of how long it takes them to complete tasks, and accuracy is monitored by spot-checking, so that error rates can be computed for each individual. Regular evaluations are conducted, and group problem-solving meetings are held monthly. Motivational techniques include shelving contests, individual goal setting, public recognition for those with no errors during the month, and the award of the prestigious title of Senior Page. Implementation of the program resulted in shelving error rates dropping from 10–16% to a remarkable 1%! This system is something many libraries may want to replicate.

Schwartz, C. "Performance Appraisal: Behavioralism and Its Discontents." *College and Research Libraries* 47 (September 1986): 438–451.

This sophisticated examination of theory and research on performance appraisal was done in order to assess the usefulness of various approaches (behavioralism, minimal model, heuristic knowledge, and in-house experimentation). The author dwells at length on what he and some others perceive to be the inadequacy of behaviorally based appraisal as a solution to the problem of rater error (which is dealt with extensively); he generally argues against the possibility (and value) of conducting objective employee appraisal. Whether he is right or not, all of this is no help for those libraries that *must* nevertheless have some sort of legally defensible appraisal system in place.

Schwartz, D., and D. Eakin. "Reference Service Standards, Performance Criteria, and Evaluation." *Journal of Academic Librarianship* 12 (March 1986): 4–8.

This very useful article describes the process of developing measurable performance criteria for librarians in a university medical library. Rejecting as too costly the methods mentioned in the literature that require surveys, tests, or observations, this staff instead decided to try to create evaluative criteria and methods that could easily be applied on an ongoing basis. They developed a list of specific behaviors which, though not quantitative or specifically measurable, were nevertheless believed to be outward indicators of performance. Initially, peer and supervisor ratings were combined to produce a composite evaluation for each individual and were used to set problem-solving goals for the coming year. Some important issues emerged, however: staff concern about introducing potentially destructive competitiveness, and the innate subjectivity of the evaluations. In response to these concerns, the peer review process was modified so that only voluntary, positive comments were submitted. Another outcome was the implementation of a reference worksheet for complicated questions, on which librarians could record what they had tried in order to answer a question, and which supervisors could review to help them evaluate staff skills. Conveys the very important point that the new system of standards worked because it was developed through staff consensus, and not imposed from above.

Seay, T., S. Seaman, and D. Cohen. "Measuring and Improving the Quality of Public Services: A Hybrid Approach." *Library Trends* 44 (January 1996): 464–490.

Although many librarians have become enamored of the quality improvement movements emanating from the business world, the authors point out that the "product" produced by a reference librarian, for example, cannot first be continuously improved until it is just right and *then* be offered to the world. Therefore, it is argued, because the quality of the service cannot be determined in advance but only after it has been delivered to the consumer, we will always be stuck with the problem of the subjective nature of reference evaluation. The pros and cons of the various methods of determining user perceptions of library services are discussed in detail. Also includes a report of the results of the regular user surveys the authors conduct in their own library, using the General User Satisfaction Survey developed by House, Weil, and McClure (1990).

September, P. "The Use of Staff Performance Appraisal in Academic Libraries." *South African Journal of Library and Information Science* 56 (June 1988): 106–119.

The author cites the forced, widespread use of institution-wide evaluation tools, designed for teaching faculty and quite inappropriate for the appraisal of librarians, as the reason for the general lack of interest in performance appraisal among academic libraries. He illustrates the advantages of a properly designed appraisal system by describing the procedures in use at two large American university libraries. The problems inherent in trying to evaluate quality versus quantity are discussed, but September (in accord with other writers whose work is mentioned) maintains that these can be overcome if staff themselves have significant input into the design of the appraisal system. The evaluation forms in use at that time at University of North Carolina at Chapel Hill and Duke University are appended; the performance criteria are generic (not specific to individual jobs).

Shroyer, A. "Toward Greater Objectivity: Formal Production Standards for Processing Units in Libraries." *Library Acquisitions* 16, no. 2 (1992): 127–134.

Proposes objective performance measures as a way to avoid common problems associated with evaluation (e.g. rater bias, inflation of scores, supervisor's reluctance to convey negative feedback, possible lawsuits). An illustrative performance standard (with specific criteria for five levels of accomplishment from Superior down to Unsatisfactory) for the task "prepares purchase orders" is included. Author stresses the need to be sure that even the higher ranges of accomplishment are actually achievable, so that workers don't end up merely frustrated, and he reminds readers that in order to be fair, all outcomes specified must be within the employee's control. He also admits that the success of such a project depends completely on the line managers who must implement it and the upper administration who must support it; if there is a problem on either of those levels, it simply won't work.

Siggins, J. *Performance Appraisal of Collection Development Librarians.* SPEC Kit 181. Washington, D.C.: Association of Research Libraries, Office of Management Services, 1992. ED 354 889.

Presents the results of a 1990 survey of over 100 ARL libraries. The documents dealing with performance criteria for bibliographers, provided by various libraries and reprinted here, would certainly be useful to large academic libraries engaged in the process of revising standards for professional staff.

Steering Committee, Central Government Library Staff. "Joint Memorandum on Review Committee on Library Staff." *Herald of Library Science* 30 (January-April 1991): 70–79.

Reports recommendations to the Indian government regarding pay scales and qualifications for librarians. Although passing reference is made to an official Indian document that apparently does contain some specific performance objectives for library personnel, this article itself does not contain any information relevant to the writing of performance standards.

Stein, D., and C. Curran. "Personnel Review: An Objectives-Based Method for Bible College Libraries." *Christian Librarian* 34 (August 1991): 112–116.

Justifies objective appraisal of personnel as the responsible stewardship of resources, and presents a rather low-key, straightforward approach to what is essentially an MBO system of personnel evaluation. Stresses the need to translate subjective traits desired into objective performance criteria, and gives examples of how to do this. A sample Employee Objectives and Review Worksheet is also included.

Stripling, B. "Quality in School Library Media Programs: Focus on Learning." *Library Trends* 44 (winter 1996): 631–656.

Although program quality is the topic, the media specialist controls many of the variables that determine quality; therefore, this article has some useful background for those working on performance standards for school librarians.

Stueart, R, and M. Sullivan. *Performance Analysis and Appraisal: A How-To-Do-It Manual for Librarians.* New York: Neal-Schuman, 1991.

Provides helpful information on the process of job analysis, an extensive treatment of the principles of performance assessment and systems, a very good list of performance descriptors for media specialists, and much more.

Subba Rao, C. "Librametry: A Statement of Limitations and Values." *Herald of Library Science* 30 (July/October 1991): 216–221.

Offers a rather arcane discussion of the measurement of library activities. Includes the human limitations that must be taken into account in setting objective work standards for various tasks, such as card filing, shelving, and bindery preparation.

Sullivan, P. "Performance Standards for SLM Centers: Taking the Initiative." *School Library Journal* 32 (May 1986): 48–49.

The author's goal is to encourage school media centers to go beyond the current practice of setting standards that are almost exclusively quantitative, to setting ones that try to measure the benefits of the programs to users. She suggests the application of ideas presented in *A Planning Process for Public Libraries* (ALA, 1980), and discusses ways in which these could be adapted to media centers.

Taylor, M., et al. "Due Process in Performance Appraisal: A Quasi-Experiment in Procedural Justice." *Administrative Science Quarterly* 40 (September 1995): 495–523.

A troubling aspect of performance appraisal is the gulf between its theoretical usefulness and the frequently expressed personal and organizational negativity toward the actual process and its effectiveness. The authors cite research suggesting that current models place managers and employees in a setting where disagreements about performance amount to disputes over who has the most accurate view of reality. Such models imply that truth can be measured against some precise standard—a highly dubious assumption, especially in service jobs where objective results are unavailable. A due-process metaphor (in which individuals are assured of fair treatment) was applied to the appraisal process in a field experiment conducted in a government agency. Results provided strong support for the positive effects of a due-process appraisal system on employees and managers. Such an approach could help reduce resistance to objective performance evaluation, particularly when the system is tied to salary and promotion. Extensive bibliography. Recommended.

Turner, A. "Appraising Support Staff: Not Just a Silly Paper Ritual." *Library Administration and Management* 4 (fall 1990): 181–183.

Rather than suggesting that the usual subjective appraisal systems that many libraries are stuck with might (or should) be changed, this author proposes work-arounds to possibly enable the hapless supervisor to turn the dreaded annual evaluation into a positive staff development experience.

Tyckoson, D. "Wrong Questions, Wrong Answers: Behavioral vs Factual Evaluation of Reference Service." *Reference Librarian*, no. 38 (1992): 151–173.

Because reference librarians so often represent the "public face" of the library, their performance is extremely important, and should be subject to objective appraisal. The author proposes a method of evaluating reference librarian effectiveness based on behavioral factors. Such a method concentrates less on the accuracy of the response and more on the process of obtaining the answer. True, reference librarians must be held accountable to patrons (both for the information provided and the manner in which it is conveyed), but Tyckoson believes that more attention should be paid to their accountability to colleagues within the institution, to administrators, and to the profession. Includes a checklist of desirable attributes, under the categories of availability, communication and search strategy skills, and attention to patrons; in addition, several different ways of making the needed observations are offered.

Verrill, P. E. "Performance Appraisal for the 1990s: Managerial Threat or Professional Right?" *British Journal of Academic Librarianship*, 8, no. 2 (1993): 98–112.

Noting that staff development has become crucial for academic libraries as managers are pressed to do more with less, the author advocates appraisal as an effective tool to help managers initiate constructive dialogue with employees for role and task clarification, target setting, and performance feedback. Following the rubric of management theorist Douglas McGregor, Verrill recommends separating performance review from salary/promotion issues in order to achieve the level of openness needed for honest communication. While admitting the difficulties, setting quantifiable measures is recommended (a few examples are given) as part of a results-oriented approach designed to give employees maximum freedom while minimizing the effects of personality factors. He is refreshingly direct in a brief discussion of the "dinosaur" problem (i.e., long-time staff whose main reasons for working are financial and/or social), and closes with an excellent analysis of the managerial issues involved in implementing a new or more rigorous appraisal system, and how to handle them.

"Virginia Beach Public Library Performance-Appraisal System Wins Awards." *Library Personnel News* 6 (November/December 1992): 2.

Announces a new performance appraisal system that incorporates principles of the Behaviorally Anchored Rating Scale, the Behavioral Expectation Scale, and the Behavioral Observation Scale. The stated object was to eliminate all trait-based terminology. For more information, contact Deborah Dunford, Virginia Beach Public Library,

4100 Virginia Beach Blvd., Virginia Beach, VA 23452, (804) 427–4057.

VonSeggern, M. "Assessment of Reference Services." *RQ* 26 (summer 1987): 487–496.

Presents a bibliography, helpfully categorized by subtopics, on the assessment of reference services.

Wallace, P. "Performance Evaluation: The Use of a Single Instrument for University Librarians and Teaching Faculty." *Journal of Academic Librarianship* 12 (November 1986): 284–290.

The problem of trying to use the same standards to evaluate teaching faculty and academic librarians with faculty status is familiar and long-standing. This article purports to analyze how such an attempt at one university had an impact on both teaching faculty and librarians. As the author indicates, however, each unit was allowed to develop additional guidelines specifying standards that would clearly reflect the uniqueness of its own discipline, so it didn't seem as though all faculty really *were* in fact evaluated by the same document. Rather, the commonality appears to have been only in the series of levels of evaluation, which were indeed the same for all. The main difficulty, as always, is the fact that librarians are typically committed to 12-month, 40-hour per week contracts, and thus have less freedom in the allocation of their time for research and publication—which calls into question the fairness of requiring the same scholarly output from them as from the teaching faculty. An abridged sample of performance standards is appended.

Webb, G. "Room for Improvement: Performance Evaluations." *Wilson Library Bulletin* 63 (February 1989): 56–57, 125.

Suggests that instead of using evaluation merely to review past performance (which cannot be changed), supervisors should concentrate more on using the appraisal as an opportunity to communicate new organizational expectations and values. After briefly mentioning common rater errors, she presents a five-phase "performance management" system designed to ensure that evaluation is an on-going and constructive process, not just a quickly forgotten annual interruption of the workflow.

Weech, T. "Who's Giving All Those Wrong Answers? Direct Service and Reference Personnel Evaluation." *Reference Librarian* (fall/winter 1984): 109–122.

Focuses on evaluation of reference service *providers*, rather than the service itself, since, at the time, the author could only identify two items in the literature dealing specifically with appraisal of reference personnel. The suggestion is made that some of the extensive methodology already available in the literature for evaluating service could perhaps be applied to personnel. Weech attempts to extrapolate some variables related to staff characteristics (education, experience, personality, searching style); however, these did not seem to correlate with number of questions answered correctly. He also reviewed the literature related to online searchers, trying to find standards that could be applied to reference staff. He touches on all the evaluative techniques in use (observation, supervisor evaluation, peer review, self- and patron evaluation) and concludes that many different sources will have to be combined to come up with more objective appraisal systems for reference librarians.

Whitmore, L. "How Are We Doing?" *Book Report* 10 (March/April 1992): 23.

A false hit on this one: rather than the expected information about school library program evaluation, the article actually pertains to informal surveying of student library aides' perceptions of their library work experience.

Womboh, B. "Performance Discrepancy in a Library Organization: The Nigerian Experience." *African Journal of Library, Archives and Information Science* 5 (April 1995): 9–18.

The author points out that industrial management techniques have long been successfully applied to some aspects of library operations; however, as many have noticed, not much attention in library literature has been given to performance, despite the fact that inadequate performance can have devastating effects on the achievement of library objectives. The author hypothesizes that the processes that make output possible are more important than the output itself, and he attempts to demonstrate this through an analysis of the causes and effects of performance discrepancy (the difference between actual performance and desired performance) in a library organization. Womboh's approach to the problem is rather different from most, and few of the problems he describes are unique to Nigeria. Very interesting.

Young, W. "Evaluating Reference Librarian." *Reference Librarian*, no. 11 (fall/winter 1984): 123–129.

Comments on the disparity between the high level of satisfaction with reference service expressed by the public and the disturbing rate of inaccurate answers provided by reference librarians (as tested by unobtrusive studies). Laments the fact that the literature does not offer much practical help in evaluating individual reference librarians, and the author makes no attempt to remedy this.

Young, W. "Methods for Evaluating Reference Desk Performance." *RQ 25* (fall 1985): 69–75.

Citing the plethora of studies already available that evaluate the effectiveness of reference service performance at the department/library level, the author addresses the need for developing reliable measures of *individual* reference desk performance—which, as he acknowledges, is uniquely difficult given the creative, idiosyncratic (and usually anonymous) nature of interactions with patrons at the reference desk. He discusses the pros and cons of MBO and unobtrusive testing as approaches to evaluation, and concludes that some combination of MBO with behavioral standards is probably the way to go: however, no specific guidance in how to do that is offered.

Zigon, J. "Oil Company Learns to Measure Work-Team Performance." *Personnel Journal* 73 (November 1994): 46–48.

Although the specific examples used in this article obviously do not apply to librarianship, the process which is described—developing criteria for measuring *group* performance—is clear and thought-provoking; it is not hard to see how such a system could at least be applied to the more "product-oriented" departments of the library (such as cataloging or acquisitions) and could also include the additional benefit of minimizing individual competitiveness within the organization.

INDEX

ABOUT THE AUTHOR

Carol Goodson is Head of the Library Access Services unit at the State University of West Georgia in Carrollton. Although she began her career more than twenty-five years ago as an academic librarian—and is now back in academic libraries again—the broad experience gained in other types of libraries between then and now helped her acquire the knowledge necessary to write this book. After leaving a position as Head of the Harriman Reserve Library at SUNY Buffalo in 1972, she worked at St. Louis Public Library (first as a reference librarian at Main, later as head of a branch); reference librarian in a special library environment at the Georgia Department of Education's Division of Public Library Services; Head of Reader's Services at Mercer University/Atlanta campus; school librarian at St. Henry School in Nashville, TN; Library Director at Aquinas Junior College in Nashville; Assistant Director and Coordinator of Children's Services for the Clayton County Public Library System in Jonesboro GA; then Coordinator of Off-Campus Library Services for West Georgia. Positions outside the library profession include community school director, retail bookstore manager, and elementary school teacher (as a member of the Dominican Sisters of Nashville).

Goodson earned a B.A. in English (1970) and M.L.S. (1972) at the State University of New York at Buffalo, and recently received the M.A. degree in English (1996) from West Georgia. In addition to work in the field of librarianship, including founding editorship of the new electronic *Journal of Library Support for Distance Education,* Goodson also maintains a scholarly interest in filmmaker Woody Allen. She is active on several committees of the American Library Association, and is a member of Phi Kappa Phi, Beta Phi Mu, Sigma Tau Delta, Omicron Delta Kappa, and the Executive Board of West Georgia's chapter of the AAUP. She may be contacted through her webpage: http://www.westga.edu/~cgoodson/.

Other Titles of Interest

HIRING LIBRARY EMPLOYEES:
A How-To-Do-It Manual
By Richard Rubin

Hiring is the single most important decision that an employer makes. This far-reaching guide covers general issues and ethical considerations; legal issues; policies and practices; effective recruitment; a 21-step implementation of the hiring process; training and orientation; and the implications of the Americans with Disabilities Act. Appendixes supply sample policies and forms, as well as a copy of the Uniform Guidelines on Employee Selection Procedures.

1-55570-159-0. 1993. 8 1/2 x 11.
209 pp. $39.95.

" . . . an outstanding practical guide to what may be the single most critical aspect of providing high-quality library service over an extended period of time." *Wilson Library Bulletin*

" . . . easily accessible and comprehensible. Library supervisors, department heads, division chairs, and directors . . . will find this invaluable." *Library Resources and Technical Services*

" . . . covers the full range of library hiring issues." *Booklist*

"Recommended for library managers and personnel departments." *Library Journal*

HUMAN RESOURCE
MANAGEMENT IN LIBRARIES:
Theory and Practice
By Richard Rubin

For libraries without a human resource specialist, this text offers the necessary expertise. All the basics are covered, including hiring, performance evaluation, compensation and benefits, and collective bargaining. Particularly valuable are discussions of employment-at-will and pay equity, and detailed information on employee turnover and the marginal employee. Each chapter concludes with a summary, and appendixes provide pertinent legislation.

1-55570-087-X. 1991. 6 x 9.
344 pp. $42.50.

"Highly recommended for every library." *Library Journal*

" . . . a very good guide to the day-to-day issues faced by administrators as human resource managers." *Information Processing & Management*

NEW EMPLOYEE
ORIENTATION:
A How-to-Do-It Manual for
Librarians
By H. Scott Davis

For a new employee, a positive work experience from the start improves attitude, confidence, and job satisfaction. For the employer, it means less turnover, faster learning, and a work force more attuned to organizational goals and norms. In this adaptable how-to, Davis combines theory and practice to help employers implement a truly effective orientation program. Chapters cover ascertaining new employees' needs; involving key participants; anticipating and handling problems; preparing for the new employee's arrival; and the orientation. Additional chapters discuss evaluation methods and participant input, and suggest ways to utilize evaluation results. A selected bibliography and an index are also included.

1-55570-158-2. 1994. 8 1/2 x 11. 144 pp. $39.95."

" . . . provides practical advice and guidance . . . " *Public Libraries*

" . . . presents a menu of program activities that can be tailored to suit the needs of many libraries." *College & Research Libraries News*

" . . . well organized and clearly written . . . practical tips are plentiful." *feliciter*

PERFORMANCE ANALYSIS AND APPRAISAL:
A How-To-Do-It Manual for Librarians
by Robert D. Stueart and Maureen Sullivan

The authors, internationally recognized authorities in library administration, offer practical advice to help supervisors at all levels evaluate staff effectively. Numerous examples and step-by-step techniques will assist supervisors in developing and writing job descriptions, analyzing jobs, preparing systematic evaluations that clarify employees" strengths and weaknesses, and establishing job enrichment specifications. Many forms and checklists are also included.

1-55570-061-6. 1991. 8 1/2 x 11. 174 pp. $42.50.

"For libraries with performance evaluation programs in place, this book will help them evaluate and strengthen them. For those wishing to establish such programs, this is the only tool to use." *Wilson Library Bulletin*

" . . . recommended to any librarian involved in performance appraisal." *Australian Library Review*

PERSONNEL ADMINISTRATION IN LIBRARIES
Second edition
Edited by Sheila Creth and Frederick Duda

Here is a practical guide examining the full range of personnel issues, including legal issues; staffing patterns; personnel planning; staff development, recruitment, and utilization; labor relations; and performance appraisals. Also covered are compensation management, personnel administration theory, and salary administration.

1-55570-036-5. 1989. 6 x 9. 353 pp. $39.95.

"Highly recommended as a resource for both personnel specialists and library professionals in general." *Library Journal*

To order or request further information, contact:
Neal-Schuman Publishers
100 Varick Street, New York, NY 10013
212-925-8650/fax toll free—1-800-584-2414
Website: http://www.neal-schuman.com